TEACH YOURSELF BOOKS

MEDITATION

TEACH YOURSELF BOOKS

MEDITATION

James Hewitt

NTC *Publishing Group*

Hodder & Stoughton

A MEMBER OF THE HODDER HEADLINE GROUP

Long-renowned as *the* authoritative source for self-guided learning – with more than 30 million copies sold worldwide – the *Teach Yourself* series includes over 200 titles in the fields of languages, crafts, hobbies, sports, and other leisure activities.

British Library Cataloguing in Publication Data
Hewitt, James
  Meditation
  1. Meditation (Teach Yourself books)
  I. Title
  158′.12 BL627
ISBN 0 340 35242 6

Library of Congress Catalog Card Number: 93–85119

First published in UK 1978 by Hodder Headline Plc, 338 Euston Road, London NW1 3BH

First published in US 1994 by NTC Publishing Group, 4255 West Touhy Avenue, Lincolnwood (Chicago), Illinois 60646 – 1975 U.S.A.

Printed and bound in Great Britain by Cox & Wyman Ltd, Reading, Berkshire,

First published 1978
20 19 18 17 16 15 14 13 12
1999 1998 1997 1996 1995 1994

Contents

Acknowledgments

The author and publishers are grateful to the following for
permission to quote copyright material:

Basil Blackwell and Mott Ltd. (Professor Ben-Ami Scharfstein,
Mystical Experience); The Buddhist Society (Bhikkhu Mangalo,
A Manual of the Practice of Recollection); Chatto and Windus
Ltd. (C. E. Montague, *A Writer's Notes on his Trade*); Con-
stable Co. Ltd. (Dom Cuthbert Butler, *Western Mysticism*);
Darton, Longman and Todd Ltd. (Dr. Una Kroll, *TM: A
Signpost for the World*); Faber and Faber Ltd. (E. Kadlovbov-
sky and G. E. H. Palmer, *Writings from the Philokalia*); Fleming
H. Revell Co. (Samuel M. Zwemer, *A Moslem Seeker after
God*); Victor Gollancz Ltd. (Victor Gollancz, *My Dear
Timothy*); T. J. S. Gray and Hong Kong University Press (Wu
Wei Wu, *Open Secret* and *The Tenth Man*); M. D. Gunasena
and Co. Ltd. (the Ven. Parawahera Vajiranana Mahathera,
Buddhist Meditation in Theory and Practice); Hamish Hamil-
ton Ltd. (Aubrey Menen, *The Space within the Heart*); Hodder
and Stoughton Ltd. and Anthony Sheil Associates Ltd. (Monica
Furlong, *Contemplating Now*); Hutchinson Publishing Group
Ltd. (Lu K'uan Yü (Charles Luk), *The Secrets of Chinese
Meditation*; Lama Anagarika Govinda, *The Way of the White
Clouds*; E. H. Shattock, *An Experiment in Mindfulness*; Profes-
sor Giuseppe Tucci, *Theory and Practice of the Mandala*; Dr.
Paul Brunton, *The Secret Path* and *The Quest for the Overself*;
J. Marquès-Rivière, *Tantrik Yoga, Hindu and Tibetan*); Alfred
A. Knopf Inc. (J. W. N. Sullivan, *Beethoven: His Spiritual
Development*); Macmillan Ltd., and the Trustees of the Tagore
Estate (Rabindranath Tagore, *Sadhana*); Methuen and Co. Ltd.
(Evelyn Underhill, *Mysticism*); William Morrow and Co. (Dr.
Herbert Benson, *The Relaxation Response*); John Murray Ltd.
(A. C. Graham, *The Book of Lieh Tzu*); New American Library

(Professor Walter T. Stace, *The Teachings of the Mystics*);
Penguin Books Ltd. (D. C. Lau, *trans.*, *Tao Te Ching*; Ernest
Wood, *Yoga*; F. C. Happold, *Mysticism*; Christmas Humphreys,
Buddhism); Sri Aurobindo Ashram (The Mother, *Bulletin*);
The Sufi Movement (Hazrat Inayat Khan, *The Way of Illumin-
ation*); Turnstone Press Ltd. (Reshad Feild, *The Last Barrier*);
Thames and Hudson Ltd. (Alan Watts, *The Way of Zen*);
Village Press (John Cowper Powys, *A Philosophy of Solitude*);
Watkins Publishing (Bishop Ignatius Brianchaninov, *On the
Prayer of Jesus*); John Weatherhill, Inc. (Katsuki Sekida, *Zen
Training*); Wildwood House Ltd. (Alan Watts, *The Supreme
Identity*).

The author would like also to thank Ronald Hutchinson for
reading the work in manuscript.

Preface

Meditation of the kind that is the subject of this book – not 'thinking about something', but pure awareness without thought – is of fast growing interest among Westerners. More than one million Europeans and Americans have been taught the most popular form of it – Transcendental Meditation. Many other Westerners are practising meditation in the manner of Indian Yoga, Theravada (southern school) Buddhism, Tibetan Buddhism, Japanese Zen Buddhism, Chinese Taoism and Islamic Sufism. Practising Christians are also experimenting with the Eastern style of meditation as part of both solitary and corporate prayer and worship.

Western interest is chiefly eclectic, involving rather an interest in the mystical essence that these traditions have in common, and in their systems of meditation, than a desire to be converted to another religion.

This book is a compendium and survey of methods of meditation as used in the religious traditions mentioned above. New adaptations tend to be clearly based on the age-old methods. In each practical chapter the basic technique is clearly given at the outset, and flesh is then added to these bare bones as the use of the method in various traditions is discussed.

Most Westerners are probably not taking up meditation for reasons solely connected with mystical goals. The good news has spread that meditation improves physical and mental health, principally by releasing stress. Medical scientists have investigated the physiological and psychological changes produced by the practice of meditation and found that it elicits a 'Relaxation Response' that is the opposite of the fight-or-flight response to danger. It is a state of deep rest and relaxation that is both different from and in many ways superior to sleep. Meditation once or twice a day, on each occasion for about twenty minutes, will lead to marked improvements in physical health and mental clarity and equanimity.

Actually the two areas – that of mystical awareness and that of psycho-physical relaxation – are not so far apart as they may at first seem. As time passes, regular deep rest and the releasing of stress through meditation affect one's whole life, leading to an intensifying and deepening of what may be broadly called 'spiritual life'. The deeply relaxed person is likely to experience an awakening of love and compassion, and an ability to appreciate more deeply the mystery and wonder of existence.

Chapters 4 to 10 of *Teach Yourself Meditation* each deal with one method of meditation, which may be employed in its basic essentials. Readers are encouraged to experiment with the methods and to find one method or combination of methods which best suits his or her approach and aims. Essentially, they are simple mental techniques such as awareness of your breathing, repeating a word in your mind, gazing at an object or visualising it in your mind, listening to a sound, sustaining loving attention, or seeing the pettiness of the ego-self. It is left to each reader to add as much or as little spiritual 'resonance' to the practice as temperament and intellectual belief make available. The validity of religious and metaphysical views has always been in question. The value of the practice of meditation is not in dispute to anyone who examines the available evidence, much of which has firm scientific basis.

JAMES HEWITT

1

Meditation for Mystical Consciousness

Why Meditate?

Until only a few years ago, if one asked the question 'Why meditate?' there would have been only one answer, which would have been something like this: 'For the spiritual and mystical purposes for which the techniques of meditation were devised and for which they have been used for thousands of years. Meditation is the spiritual training of the world's religions and serves the supreme goals of those religions. Though there is some variation in the doctrines and dogmas of these religions, and in the words employed to describe their goals, these goals may be summed up under the single description of mystical consciousness. The answer to the question "Why meditate?" is therefore – *to attain mystical consciousness*.'

This kind of answer is still the response in the East, and applies to many of the people who take up meditation in the West, where there has been in recent years an enormous growth of interest in the Eastern religions of Hinduism, Buddhism (including Zen), Taoism and Sufism, the mystical wing of Islam. Each of these religions has meditation at the centre of its spiritual training. There has also been greater interest in Christian contemplative prayer, which parallels the kind of meditation found in the Eastern religions.

But today, in the West at any rate, a second reason for meditating may be given, and this is the one which applies to the majority of meditators. It is that word has spread that meditation of the Eastern kind improves physical and mental health by inducing psycho-physical rest and relaxation of a depth and power of refreshment that is in some ways superior to that of sleep. Before showing how medical scientists have recorded physiological changes in meditators which confirm this claim, we will first look at the traditional mystical reason for meditating.

Meditation and the Religions

In the East, meditation as a way of altering consciousness is a revered tradition which has greatly influenced the cultures of India, China, Tibet, Japan, Burma, Thailand and other countries. In these cultures there is no doubt that the goal of meditation is 'mystical' or 'higher' consciousness. The methods of meditation described in this book, however they are used and for whatever purposes, originated within the major religions, principally those of the East. When meditation is used, as it is today in the West, for improved health and physical and mental relaxation, or as a psychotherapy, it will be found that the methods used are either basic techniques of the Eastern religions or are obviously based upon them.

All the major religions advise the practice of meditation.

HINDUISM

Whoever here among men attain greatness,
*   they have, as it were, part of the reward of meditation.*
*   Reverence meditation.*
He who reverences meditation as the Supreme –
*   as far as meditation goes,*
*   so far he has unlimited freedom.*

Chandogya Upanishad

JAINISM

He who is rich in control renounces everything
*   and meditates on the reflections on life.*
He whose soul is purified by meditating
*   is compared to a ship in water.*

Like a ship reaching the shore, he gets beyond misery.

Sutra-Kritanga Sutra

SIKHISM

The world is an ocean, and difficult to cross.
* How shall man traverse it?*
As a lotus in the water remaineth dry,
* As also a water-fowl in the stream —*
So by meditating on the Word
* Shalt though be unaffected by the world.*

Guru Nanak

TAOISM

I do my utmost to attain emptiness;
I hold firmly to stillness.
The myriad creatures all rise together
And I watch their return.
The teeming creatures
All return to their separate roots.
Returning to one's roots is known as stillness.

Tao Te Ching (translated by D. C. Lau)

BUDDHISM

* The Noble Eightfold Path:*
Right Understanding
Right Thoughts or Motives
Right Speech
Right Action
Right Means of Livelihood
Right Moral Effort
Right Concentration or Mindfulness
Right Meditation

JUDAISM

God wants the heart.

The Talmud

CHRISTIANITY

*Neither shall they say, Lo here! or, lo there! for,
behold, the kingdom of God is within you.*

St. Luke 17:21

ISLAM

*Meditate on thy Lord in thine own mind
  with humility and without loud speaking,
evening and morning,
  And be not one of the negligent.*

The Koran

Hinduism

Hinduism, India's national religion, has no founder and no book such as the Bible to provide a source of divine revelation. The religion grew gradually over a period of five thousand years. It has been described, by Sir Charles Eliot, as 'a jungle, not a building'. The result of its development is that it tolerates the widest possible viewpoints: polytheism, monotheism, monism, pantheism, panantheism and so on. The Hindu scriptures contradict each other and themselves without unease. Mysticism at its purest is found in the ancient *Upanishads*. Systematised meditation within Hinduism, with the aim of attaining mystical union, developed as Yoga.

The classic Yoga text on meditation is Patanjali's *Yoga Sutras*, written about 200–300 BC, in which he describes the 'eight limbs of Yoga', which remain even today the foundations of mainstream practice. The first and second limbs are, respectively, moral abstinences and observances. The third limb is posture, the most important for meditation being that of sitting in a comfortable position with the back erect. Several cross-legged sitting postures are identified with the practice of meditation, of which the most famous is the Lotus Posture. We will be describing sitting postures for meditation in Chapter 3. The fourth limb is breath control. Where meditation is concerned, this mainly means breathing gently, smoothly, and regularly. There are close links between rapid, jerky breathing and excitement and between slow, smooth breathing and tranquillity. The fifth limb of Yoga is sense-withdrawal, turning attention away from the bombardment of sense stimuli so as to place attention on the object of meditation. Dwelling upon the object is concentration, the sixth limb. When the current of unified attention flows steadily and effortlessly, this is meditation or contemplation, the seventh limb. The culminating stage is *samadhi*, which is the state of pure existence and being. In terms of Hindu mysticism, the meditator in the eighth stage knows his essential Self beyond the ego, and Self (*Atman*) is identical with Brahman, the all-pervading universal spirit or Overself. This union is the supreme goal of Hindu meditation and mysticism.

The equating of Self and Brahman is the central message of the *Upanishads*, the first of which were written between 800 and 500 BC, in prose and verse of great beauty and spirituality. The identity of individual spirit and universal spirit is summed up in the much quoted phrase *tat tvam asi* – 'that thou art'. Meditation is recommended as a practice for realising universal being. The *Svetasvatara Upanishad* says: 'Like butter or cream is the Self in everything. Knowledge of the Self is gained through meditation. This is Brahman.'

The philosophy of the *Upanishads* is called Vedanta, the *anta* or 'end' of the *Vedas*, the earliest Hindu scriptures. Many Westerners have admired the beauty and thought and expression of the *Upanishads*, as they have the later *Bhagavad Gita* or Song of the Lord, written about 300 BC. In it Lord Krishna instructs Arjuna in the various Yoga paths. There is said to be a Yoga to suit every temperament.

Brahman is the One of world mysticism. Every major religion has its terms to describe mystical consciousness and its practices to uncover it. Here the influence of Yoga meditation is everywhere apparent.

Buddhism

Buddhism arose in India about 2,500 years ago, at a time when Hinduism had in some eyes degenerated into scholasticism and arid adherence to ritual. Gautama Siddhartha forsook princely wealth and privilege to search for a way to end the unhappiness of mankind. After asceticism had failed, meditation brought the answer. Following his experience of enlightenment, Gautama Siddhartha was known as the Buddha, meaning 'Enlightened One'. Buddhism is primarily a religion of enlightenment. There is no concept of God in Buddhism, and the Buddha is not a god, though statues of the Buddha may become aids to meditation. There is no more potent symbol of Eastern meditation than the serene face of the meditating Buddha.

The Buddha taught that to live is to experience three conditions: change or impermanence (*anicca*), the unreality of the ego-self (*anatta*), and suffering (*dukkha*). 'One thing do I teach,' he said, '*Dukkha* and deliverance from *dukkha*.' *Dukkha* is usually translated as suffering but it refers in its widest sense to the feeling of dissatisfaction caused by living out of harmony with one's essential nature and that of the universe.

There are two main schools of Buddhism: the northern, found in Tibet, China, and Japan, and the southern or Theravada school, found in Sri Lanka, Burma, Thailand, and other countries in south-east Asia. The scriptures of the northern school are written in Sanskrit and those of the southern school are in Pali. Tibetan Buddhist meditation contains some pre-Buddhist elements and has an exotic and dramatic quality. Several centres for the practice of Tibetan Buddhist meditation were set up in Europe and in America after Tibetan monks fled to the West on the invasion of their country by the Chinese. The Buddhism of China and Japan is the direct school of Zen (Chinese, Ch'an). The Theravada school favours a gradual approach to enlightenment and makes much use of the method of 'mindfulness' as a way to insight. Right Mindfulness is number seven in the Noble Eightfold Path and Right Meditation is number eight.

The Buddhist view is that 'Buddha-mind' or 'Buddha-nature' is latent in everyone, and meditation has the capacity to uncover it. The goal of the Buddhist mystic way is Nirvana, which is not annihilation but blissful liberation from identification with the pseudo-ego.

Taoism

China never had a unified religion – but Confucianism, Taoism, and Buddhism have all had a large following. Chinese reverence for nature reaches its most aesthetic and philosophical expression in Taoism. To be in harmony with the rhythms and natural laws of the universe – that is, with the Tao – is the highest goal. The Tao (pronounced 'Dow') is impossible to translate, but it is often translated as 'way' or 'nature'. It is the principle of order in the universe. In it the *yin* and the *yang*, the dark and the light, the feminine and the masculine, principles in the universe merge and interact in single harmony. The chief symbol of the Tao is water, which finds its own level. The Taoist should live simply and effortlessly, as water flows. Similar ideas are found in Zen, in which there has been considerable Taoist influence.

Taoism received its most beautiful and profound expression in the *Tao Te Ching* by Lao Tzu, whose name literally means 'Old Master'. The facts about him are in doubt, but one source places his birth in 604 BC. The second key work in philosophical Taoism is the *Book of Chuang Tzu,* who is said to have lived in the fourth century BC. His book is a collection of essays and stories. He wrote: 'I do good to those who do me good, and to those who do not do me good, and thus it is well with everyone.' Happiness and freedom are achieved by dispensing with those things which cause unhappiness and bondage. Taoism is known as 'The Method of Losing'. Lao Tzu said: 'To search for knowledge is to gain day by day; to search for Tao is to lose day by day.'

The Taoism of Lao Tzu and Chuang Tzu is known as 'philosophical Taoism' to distinguish it from Taoism as a popular religion, which degenerated into the pursuit of immortal life and psychic powers. In philosophical Taoism we have one of the finest flowers of Oriental mystical philosophy – and the creative source of Zen. It is often said, with justification, that the continuation of philosophical Taoism is to be found in Ch'an and Zen and not in popular religious Taoism.

Zen

Buddhism was shaped by the practical Chinese mind and by contact with Taoism into a form that was sturdy and direct, and by late in the eighth century AD it had taken individual form in the school of Ch'an, or Zen in Japanese. A much quoted summary of its approach is: 'A direct transmission (of Enlightenment) outside the scriptures; no dependence on words and letters; direct pointing to the soul of man; seeing into one's self-nature and attaining Buddhahood.' The words Ch'an and Zen are forms of the Sanskrit *dhyana*, meaning meditation.

Soto and Rinzai are the two main schools of Zen. In Soto Zen, sitting meditation is itself the goal and the practice is described as *shikantaza* or 'just sitting'. Rinzai employs *zazen*, literally 'sitting Zen', and also uses the *koan* – such as the famous 'what is the sound of one hand clapping?' – which is a kind of nonsense riddle that disorientates linear thought. A similar purpose is behind the non-logical replies of Zen masters to the questions of their pupils, in the question-and-answer sessions called *mondo*.

The Zen term for sudden illumination is *satori* or *kensho*. Meditation prepares the mind for its appearance, which may be at an unlikely moment. In Zen literature stories are told of its being triggered by the sound of a pebble striking bamboo, the glimpse of a flower, a slap from a master or the sight of him eating his rice.

Sufism

The Sufis have existed as a mystical group within Islam for many centuries, but they claim that Sufism is the essence of all religions. Hazrat Inayat Khan, who took the teachings of Sufism to Europe and America in 1910, taught: 'It should be now clear that Sufism does not add another community to the number of castes and creeds which already exist. Any person can study Sufism, and make use of it for guidance in daily life without discarding his existing associations with other communities. As he perceives the underlying wisdom, he perceives also that he is related to every other community, and he is at one with them in the path of love and light.' (*The Way of Illumination*, The Sufi Movement, Geneva).

Sufi poets, mainly Persian, have produced the world's finest body of mystical poetry. Its characteristic tone is intoxication with love of God. Jalal al-Din Rumi (1207–1273) is probably the greatest of these poets, though Omar Khayyam is more widely known in the West through a poem by Edward Fitzgerald, which, however fine as a poem, should not be thought of as authentic Sufism.

The goal of Sufism is 'universal man', transcending all cultural and credal differences. The real essence in man is the product of the universe in evolution. The Sufi develops from stage to stage in a spiritual ascent. Finally there is liberation from the ego-self and he steps into the freedom of the cosmic-self. The concept of cosmic consciousness appears in other mystical traditions. The similarity to Hindu Vedanta, Taoism, and Buddhism in its various schools is clear. But the Sufi worships a personal God and not an impersonal Absolute, and in its intensity of loving attention and use of prayer Sufism has close affinities with Judaic and Christian mysticism.

Judaism

Jewish mysticism, like that of Sufism and Christianity, aims at union with God. An early form of Jewish mystical practice is that of Merkabolism, which can be traced to the first century AD, but Hasidism has had the greatest and most lasting influence. There are similarities with Zen and with Sufism in the Hasidic emphasis on the perfected man, whose presence alone is a form of instruction. Of one Hasid, a disciple said: 'I did not go to him to learn Torah from him but to watch him tie up his boot-laces.'

Reciting the names of God has been a much practised form of meditation in Jewish mysticism. The letters of God's name have played a role that has similarities to the use of OM, the primary word, by the Hindu Yogis, and of 'Allah' by the Sufis. Control of posture and breath parallels similar practices in Yoga. Gershom G. Scholem, in *Jewish Mysticism* (Shocken Books, New York) says that the teachings of Rabbi Abulafia 'represents but a Judaized version of that ancient spiritual technique which has found classical expression in the practices of the Indian mystics who follow the system known as *Yoga.*'

Christianity

Christian contemplative prayer parallels some Eastern methods of meditation. In its most mystical development it goes beyond words and images to pure transcendental consciousness. Some similarities to Yoga methods in breath control and repetition of prayers is found in the contemplative techniques of the Christian mystics, in particular as part of the Eastern Orthodox tradition.

But the Christian contemplative 'way' to union with God is that of loving attention, which parallels a similar devotional approach in Sufism and in Bhakti Hinduism.

More information on the characters and beliefs of the above systems of mystical meditation will be given in the chapters to follow. There is now a large literature on the Eastern religions published in the West, some indication of which will be found in the bibliography at the end of this book.

Mystical Consciousness

The aims of meditation in the religions mentioned above have to do with enlightenment about the meditator's essential nature and that of Ultimate Reality, with union with God or the Absolute (Ultimate Reality again), with states of consciousness 'higher' than those with which we are all familiar – dreamless sleep, dreaming sleep, and normal waking consciousness. All in all, meditation has been practised for thousands of years and is still practised today as a way of uncovering mystical consciousness. We say 'uncovering' mystical consciousness, because the great mystical traditions agree that the field of pure being is latent in everyone, all of the time – only illusion and ignorance (ignore-ance) prevent us realising it. Seeing reality, who or what we are, we are transformed and liberated into a state of freedom which Hindus call *moksha*, Taoists call living in harmony with the Tao, Buddhists call Nirvana, Sufis call universal man, and Christians call the unitive life.

'Mystical' is one of those words that defies being defined in one way that will satisfy everyone. The following definition by Olaf Stapleton seems more straightforward and comprehensive than most: 'In the stricter sense, the word "mystical" applies to a special kind of non-rational experience, in which, it is claimed, the individual attains some degree of illumination or insight into the essential and normally hidden nature of reality. This insight is reported to be not merely a kind of knowing; it is the supreme achievement of knowing-feeling-striving in one all-fulfilling act. The "knowing" aspect of it is said to be not abstract, like intellectual knowing, but concrete, like sense-experience. In fact, in so far as it is knowledge, it is an immediate acquaintance with the hidden essence of a "reality" which is said to lie behind all ordinary and illusory experience.' (*Philosophy and Living*, volume 2, Penguin Books).

Mystical experience is generally accepted as supreme truth in the East. In the West, many people are uncomfortable about it, or sceptical. Mysticism is widely misunderstood in the West. Much of the antipathy to it evaporates on closer examination of the character of mainstream mysticism. It is often wrongly identified with things 'mysterious' and 'misty', because of the similarity of the words. Reading an anthology of mystical writings by mystics of many cultures – such as Plotinus, Shankgara, St. John of the Cross, St. Teresa of Avila, Meister Eckhart, Lao Tzu, Rumi, and so on – will wring from even a sceptic an acknowledgement that mystical writings make a considerable contribution to literature, to the exploration of human consciousness, and to the attempt by man to wrest from the universe its innermost secrets. Professor Walter T. Stace's *The Teachings of the Mystics* (New American Library) is such an anthology, and it has a valuable introduction on 'What Is Mysticism' by Professor Stace, whose approach is sympathetic to mysticism and at the same time rational and clear-headed. Such a collection shows that the mystics of East and West are in agreement on the essential components of the *experience* of mystical consciousness. That such experiences have been known in many cultures and in all ages is undeniable. But we must distinguish between the experience and its interpretation. A Christian may view mystical consciousness in terms of the Trinity (though Meister Eckhart is virtually in accord with the Eastern philosophies in speaking of 'the God beyond God'); a Buddhist will say he has found 'Buddha-mind' or the 'Void'; the Hindu will speak of Self being Brahman, the cosmic spirit; and so on.

It is difficult to rationalise by the use of language a mystical experience; one can describe light in terms of dark, high in terms of low and hot in terms of cold but one cannot describe a mystical experience in this way because there is no known opposite against which to set it. The juxtaposition of qualities upon which language is based has apparently been transcended, and mystics naturally turn to the concepts supplied by their religions and cultures – what William James usefully called the mystic's 'overbelief'. In *The Varieties of Religious Experience* (Long-mans, Green), James wrote: 'The fact is that the mystical feeling of enlargement, union and emancipation has no specific intellectual content whatever of its own. It is capable of forming matrimonial alliances with material furnished by the most diverse philosophies and theology, provided only they can find a place in their framework for its peculiar emotional mood.'

Professor Stace points out in *The Teachings of the Mystics* that the mystical experience is one of an 'undifferentiated unity' and that 'there seems to be nothing religious about an undifferentiated unity as such.' Why then is mystical experience nearly always associated with religion? Professor Stace suggests it is because the experience is usually one of 'melting away' and passing into infinite being. There is, too, a sense of being beyond space and beyond time. A third association between mystical consciousness and religion is its heightened feelings of bliss, peace, and joy. Professor Stace is led to say: 'Thus we see that mysticism naturally, though not necessarily, becomes associated with whatever is the religion of the culture in which it appears. It is, however, important to realise that it does not favour any particular religion.'

There are mystics who, like Richard Jefferies, stay outside the framework of religious ideas – though it may be argued that all mystical experience is religious in the broadest definition of the word.

The Main Characteristics of Mystical Consciousness

Several writers who have made studies of mystical experience have attempted to set out all of its characteristics. Professor Ben-Ami Scharfstein, in *Mystical Experience* (Basil Blackwell), gives eleven characteristics: 'sameness; separation; uniqueness; inclusion; family strangeness; depletion; aggression; conscience; mirror-reversal; humour; reality.' Aggression is a surprising inclusion, but refers to the mystic's self-conquest and the exclusion of the world from consciousness. Humour does not feature, it seems to me, in all mystical experience, but appears as a belly-laugh in Zen and in Sufism in some of the 'teaching stories', especially those concerning the comic character Nasrudin.

Professor Scharfstein acknowledges that there is overlapping between his characteristics. Most modern writers, when space is limited, are happy to fall back on William James's four characteristics. Passivity, his fourth characteristic, has an important role in the manner in which we meditate: meditation is most effective when there is passive awareness.

William James's four characteristics are:

1. *Ineffability*. The mystic finds himself or herself unable to describe the exact nature of the meditative experience in such a way that others can recreate the experience in their minds. As I mentioned above, language works on the basis of contrasting the qualities of things to which the words refer (i.e. hot and cold), but mystical consciousness transcends the opposites. The state must be directly experienced. 'In this peculiarity mystical states are more like states of feeling than like states of intellect,' says James. 'No one can make clear to another who has never had a certain feeling, in what the quality or worth of it consists.'

2. *Noetic quality*. There is an element of *knowing* about the experience, yet it goes beyond knowledge accumulated by the discursive intellect. The mystical traditions speak of 'insight' and 'enlightenment' or 'illumination'. The illumination is charged with a sense of certainty. Professor James fails to mention the powerful sense of Oneness and Unity that strikes with directness and immediacy, so that the mystic feels he has broken through to what really is, to Reality with a capital 'R'. Such is the strength and immensity of the experience that the mystic is filled with awe and wonder that is easily channelled into religious feeling and belief.

3. *Transiency*. The experience is usually of short duration.

4. *Passivity*. James writes: 'Although the oncoming of mystical states may be facilitated by preliminary voluntary operations, as by fixing the attention, or going through certain bodily performances, or in other ways which manuals of mysticism prescribe; yet when the characteristic sort of consciousness has once set in, the mystic feels as if he were grasped and held by a superior power.'

Another characteristic of mystical experience that should be mentioned is that the life of the mystic is usually transformed, becoming more egoless, more joyful and loving.

The Thirst For the Infinite

A thirst for the infinite, for cosmic consciousness, for union with God or the Absolute, has possessed many minds in many cultures for thousands of years. Some have taken their place in the story of mankind as saints, some as reformers, some as founders or leaders of religions, and some as poets, artists, and musicians. But most remain unknown. They exist today just as they have in every age. They have been described in the following words by Evelyn Underhill, in her monumental study *Mysticism* (Methuen):

'The most highly developed branches of the human family have in common one peculiar characteristic. They tend to produce – sporadically it is true, and often in the teeth of adverse external circumstances – a curious and definite type of personality; a type which refuses to be satisfied with that which other men call experience, and is inclined, in the words of its enemies, to "deny the world in order that it may find reality." We meet these persons in the East and in the West; in the ancient, medieval, and modern worlds. Their one passion appears to be the prosecution of a certain spiritual and intangible quest: the finding of a "way out" or a "way back" to some desirable state in which alone they can satisfy their craving for absolute truth. This quest, for them, has constituted the whole meaning of life. They have made for it, without effort, sacrifices which have appeared enormous to other men: and it is an indirect testimony to its objective actuality that, whatever the place or period in which they have arisen, their aims, doctrines and methods have been substantially the same. Their experience, therefore, forms a body of evidence, curiously self-consistent and often mutually explanatory, which must be taken into account before we can add up the sum of the energies and potentialities of the human spirit, or reasonably speculate on its relations to the unknown world which lies outside the boundaries of sense.'

Any reader who hears the call of absolute reality as an undying note will not need to be persuaded to meditate: and he or she will not have the slightest doubt about why they meditate. But there are less controversial reasons for meditating, to which we will turn in the following chapter.

2

Meditating for Better Health
and for
Psycho-physiological Relaxation

Rewarding Meditation

Any person who has meditated regularly for some months in any of the ways described in this book will probably have known and welcomed the relaxing effect it has had on body and mind. The nervous system has released stress and become more stable. Capacity to cope with stressful situations has been enhanced. Body and mind have more energy, and consciousness has more clarity.

There are other psycho-physiological changes. The regular meditator needs less sleep and goes to sleep without the aid of pills or goes to sleep less tired and awakes more refreshed, while having the same amount of sleep as before. The muscles have 'let go' from tension and there may be a feeling of lightness and buoyancy, especially just after meditating. In the meditation training centres in Burma and Thailand, monks and lay persons practising mindfulness of breathing alternating with mindfulness (bare awareness) of activity -- that is, practising sitting meditation and mobile meditation through most of the day -- find they need only about four hours sleep. Concentration improves and is effortless, which is hardly surprising since the nature of this meditation may be described as 'effortless concentration', 'effortless attention', or 'effortless awareness'. Being more at ease with oneself and the universe leads to easier personal relationships. Love and compassion flower in the expansion of being that follows the lifting of contracting tensions. Living becomes more flowing and non-volitional, and at the same time more joyful and fulfilling. There are more ego-transcending 'peak experiences'.

These may seem excessive claims for the practice of what are often very simple mental techniques, but they are supported by the evidence of investigation by medical scientists.

These psycho-physiological changes have been known to meditators for thousands of years. As most meditation took place in a religious context, in a conceptual rather than organisational sense for the solitary meditator, in a forest hut or a mountain cave, these changes were of minor importance in themselves, though welcomed as aids to spiritual progress. It is only in recent years, when the physiological and psychological changes in meditators have been studied with the use of intricate electrical machines, that the effects of regular meditation on body and mind have been documented and taken from their religious and spiritual context and been looked at as something worthy of attention in themselves. For the man or woman on the path of mystical unfoldment they are secondary, though welcome; but for many thousands of tensed Westerners today they bring the good news that techniques as simple as sitting comfortably and letting attention flow with the breath or mentally repeating a word will bring rest and refreshment that is superior in several respects to that produced by sleep.

The Relaxation Response

Prominent in discovering the ways in which meditation improves physical and emotional health and helps the individual deal more effectively with stress has been Dr. Herbert Benson, of the Harvard Medical School, who has said that the response of the human organism to traditional methods of meditation and new adaptations, when four simple components are present, is as marked and as automatic as the well-known fight-or-flight response with which the human organism meets a dangerous situation. He reported his findings in several papers for medical journals and in his book *The Relaxation Response* (William Morrow, New York).

Dr. Benson's study of practitioners of Transcendental Meditation, combined with that movement's widespread publicity in the mass media, spread news of the Relaxation Response to meditation.

The main physiological features of the response are as follows:

The heart rate of meditators decreases by, on average, about three beats per minute.

The rate of breathing decreases.

The body's consumption of oxygen decreases, by as much as twenty per cent, which means that there is a marked decrease in the body's rate of metabolism. Similar hypometabolism occurs only in deep sleep and in hibernation – but meditators show different physiological changes to those of sleep and hibernation.

Blood lactate decreases. Lactate is a substance produced by the metabolism of the skeletal muscles. High levels of lactate in the blood are associated with attacks of anxiety.

Blood pressure is at normal levels. Dr. Benson found that meditation reduces blood pressure in individuals who have high blood pressure before starting meditation.

The brain produces alpha and perhaps theta waves, in patterns and distribution different from that of deep sleep or hypnosis. When the brain is active it records beta waves – alpha waves are slower and linked with states of relaxation; theta waves are slower still.

Dr. Benson soon became aware that he had discovered 'an integrated response opposite to the fight-or-flight response and one which was in no way unique to Transcendental Meditation (the method employed by the people he first studied). Indeed, lowered oxygen consumption, heart rate, respiration, and blood lactate are indicative of decreased activity of the sympathetic nervous system and represent a hypometabolic, or restful, state. On the other hand, the physiological changes of the fight-or-flight response are associated with increased sympathetic nervous system activity and represent a hypermetabolic state.'

Some of the physiological changes of the Relaxation Response can be elicited by such Western techniques of relaxation as autogenic training, progressive relaxation, and hypnosis. But these methods, in their earlier stages at any rate, require an instructor and lengthy training to reach the stage of deep relaxation. On the other hand, meditation is practised by oneself usually, can be self-taught, and is easily learned. Moreover, good results come from the start.

Which forms of meditation trigger the Relaxation Response? Dr. Benson's investigation shows that the traditional methods – such as those described in this book – can evoke the Relaxation Response. They will be effective, he says, as long as they contain four basic elements. These are: a quiet environment; an object for the attention to dwell upon; a passive attitude (the most important component); and a comfortable posture, usually sitting.

The altered state of consciousness associated with the Relaxation Response is that described in the literature of religious and secular mysticism. Dr. Benson writes of the 'age-old universality of this altered state of consciousness', which he supports by quotations primarily from the religious literature of many cultures.

Meditation as Mental Hygiene

There has been a great deal of investigation into the physiological and the psychological effects of meditation, most of which has concentrated on Transcendental Meditation – in which the technique is mentally to repeat a Sanskrit word (a *mantra*). Practitioners of Transcendental Meditation make good subjects because they are not isolated in any way from society and TM, as it is known, is very simple. Maharishi Mahesh Yogi has full confidence in his method of meditation and welcomes scientific investigation.

The outcome of these studies is that it would appear that meditation helps people break addictions, become more efficient in many ways, cope well with stress, and move in the direction of more spontaneous and fulfilled living. Tests taken before and after meditating for a short time showed greater progress towards self-actualisation in meditators. Self-actualisation is a term used by some psychologists, principally A. H. Maslow, to denote the tendency of the human organism to fulfil its higher potentialities as lower needs are satisfied. Self-actualising people represent the psychologically most healthy people in society, says Professor

Maslow. They have 'B' – for Being – values, and they more frequently have 'peak experiences'. 'B' values, according to Professor Maslow in *Towards a Psychology of Being* (Van Nostrand, Princeton, N.J.), include wholeness, perfection, completion, simplicity, uniqueness, effortlessness, truth, honesty, reality – the values one would expect in the 'universal man' aimed for by the mystics. And 'peak experiences' are marked by 'total attention', perceiving 'the whole of Being', 'ego transcendence', and other hallmarks of mystical consciousness. 'The peak-experience of pure delight are for my subjects among the ultimate goals of living and the ultimate validations and justifications for it.'

Meditation is clearly a mental hygiene – and mystical experience, it seems, has varying degrees of intensity and may not be as rare as most people suppose.

3

How to Meditate –
Poised Posture, Poised Breathing,
Poised Awareness

It seems to me that there are six main requirements for beneficial meditation:

1. A place in which to meditate where the distractions of noise, nearness of other people, movement, light, and so on are within your tolerance level.
2. Physical and mental comfort. Minor discomforts may not have enough intensity to mar the quality of meditation.
3. A sitting posture that is poised and comfortable.
4. Quiet, gentle, smooth, and regular breathing.
5. A meditation object or stimulus on which the attention may dwell. It has to be available for about twenty minutes.
6. Poised awareness.

Where to Meditate

A quiet and pleasant place in your home is the best place to meditate regularly, a place where there is the maximum freedom from distraction by other people, noise, currents of air, flashing lights, and so on. In these matters some people have a higher tolerance level than others. Some meditators develop the ability to meditate amid a certain amount of bustle and noise, on trains, on buses, on a seat in the park, in a city square and so on. But a quiet, pleasant room at home is the preference of most meditators. If there is a telephone in the room, take it off the hook.

Physical and Mental Comfort

Again individual tolerance levels vary. Physical pain or mental distress are clearly disruptive and may make meditation impossible. In normal circumstances there is much you can do to add to your comfort and prepare yourself to sit down for meditation.

It is helpful to take a bath or to wash your hands and face at least; to blow your nose; to brush your teeth and rinse out your mouth with water; to splash your eyes with cold water. Empty your bladder and your bowels too if possible.

Wear loose-fitting clothing. Ties, belts, and anything constricting should be taken off or loosened. Take off your shoes. But wear sufficient clothing to prevent your body becoming cold.

Unless your nostrils are blocked, breathe through them and keep your mouth closed. Some traditions say that the tip of the tongue should touch the palate during meditation; others say that the tip of the tongue should be against the back of the upper teeth; others say that the tip of the tongue should be touching the back of the lower teeth and the tongue lies flat in the mouth. The third position, with the tip of the tongue against the lower teeth, seems to me the most natural – but you should place your tongue in whatever way you find most comfortable. You may never have given it a thought if I had not mentioned it.

A copious flow of saliva in the mouth is one of the marks of deep relaxation: if you feel a desire to swallow, then swallow. The same applies to an itch – scratch it and go back to meditating.

Should the eyes be open or closed? If you are meditating by gazing at some object in the environment then your eyes will be open at that time, though closed for inner visualisation of the object. Normally, however, it is best to close the eyes during meditation, thereby cutting out myriad visual stimuli and helping the attention turn inwards. Closing the eyes is a simple but important step in what Patanjali, the 'Father of Yoga', called *pratyahara* or 'sense-withdrawal'.

It is true that Zen Buddhists keep the eyes partly open during *zazen* ('sitting meditation') and rest their gaze on a spot on the floor a few feet in front of them. This may have some influence on certain elements of extravertive mysticism in Zen, in which the external environment is seen in a new light at enlightenment (*satori*). Zen monks may meditate for hours and keeping the eyes partly open prevents their falling asleep. It is significant that Katsuki Sekida, in *Zen Training* (John Weatherhill, New York) – in which he instructs in how to meditate in the Zen manner at home – goes against tradition and instructs that the eyes should be closed.

The Best Times to Meditate

Best results are obtained from meditation when it is practised once or twice a day. For most people, twice a day is superior to once a day. Allow at least two hours to pass following a meal: meditation is rarely comfortable shortly after a meal.

To take best advantage from meditating twice a day, meditate in the morning before breakfast and again in the evening before dinner. Separating the two sessions by at least six hours makes full use of meditation's capacity to recharge energies. If you meditate once a day, mid-afternoon or early evening is a good time, though not convenient for everyone. You may prefer to meditate before breakfast.

How Long Should I Sit?

If you are leading a normal active life and have not become a recluse, then you should meditate for about twenty minutes each session, though between ten and thirty minutes is effective. Beginners may peep at a clock to see when the time is up, but after some practice the body's inbuilt clock usually lets the meditator know when the twenty minutes is up.

Do not get up abruptly. Open your eyes and sit quietly for a minute or two before rising to your feet. Carry the relaxation of meditation into your subsequent movements. The more you keep up your daily practice of meditation, the more the valuable quality of meditative relaxation will infuse every activity throughout the day.

POISED POSTURE

It is not essential for the meditator to sit in one of the Eastern cross-legged postures, but they are well worth mastering, even if only in one of the simpler positions. The Eastern cross-legged sitting postures have been associated with the practice of meditation from antiquity. They are so effective because of the inter-relatedness of body posture and states of consciousness. The Eastern sages who formulated the practices of meditation found that poise of body favoured poise of mind. There are certain practical considerations too that make the classic postures of meditation so effective. It is essential that the meditator should not fall asleep, nor should he topple forwards, backwards, or to one side. The classic cross-legged postures ensure that the body is stable and immobile, with the psycho-physical energies gathered together and harmonised – that is, they provide the ideal bodily counterpart for meditative awareness. The feeling engendered, provided the meditator is comfortable in the pose, is one of firm-ness, symmetry, balance, and poise. The nervous system is toned. The back is kept easily upright – considered essential in sitting for meditation – the blood circulates freely in the abdomen, the spine, and the brain, and it is easy to breathe deeply and freely into the abdomen. The centre of gravity in the body becomes established a little below the navel – the region called the *tanden* by the Japanese and considered to be 'the vital centre'.

However, meditation can be fully effective if the meditator sits on a chair, as long as three essentials are met: the back should be erect, though without rigidity, and the body must be comfortable and immobile.

Tomio Hirai, a Japanese psychiatrist, reports in *Zen Medi-tation Therapy* (Japan Publications, Tokyo) how tests were made of the body movements of Zen priests, 'ordinary' people, and neurotics. Restlessness was measured with a device using a suspended lead weight with an inked tip which recorded move-ments on white paper. The difference between the movements of the Zen priests, the 'ordinary' persons, and the neurotics were recorded as a small asterisk, a larger one, and a much larger one.

The cross-legged poses are made easier and more comfortable if you sit on a cushion, which should be firm and not soft and lumpy. A thin cushion, folded cloth or mat may be placed under the knees. Special cushions are made for use by Zen Buddhists:

they are illustrated in Philip Kapleau's *The Three Pillars of Zen* (Beacon Press, Boston).

Egyptian Posture (Sitting on a chair)

This is simply sitting on a straight-backed chair. Sit firmly on the sitting bones, rocking backwards and forwards and from side to side a few times to locate the point of balance where the weight most fully presses on the chair seat. Beginners will find that placing the fingers beneath the buttocks will help locate the points of maximum pressure from the sitting bones. The fingers are then

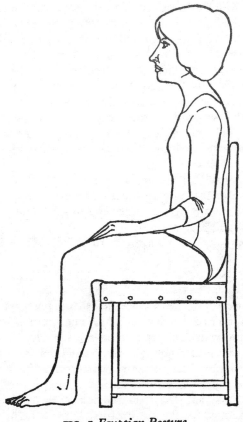

FIG. 1 *Egyptian Posture*

withdrawn and the hands cupped in the lap, the back of the left hand on the right palm (but reversed if you are left-handed), or the right palm may be placed on the right thigh and the left palm on the left thigh in line with the right hand. Cupping the hands in the manner indicated might be called the 'Buddhist' position. The point about placing the left hand on top of the right is that it feels more satisfactory to cover and immobilise the most active hand (so right hand on left for left-handed people).

Sit tall with the back straight, though poised rather than rigid. The head should be in line with the spine and the chin kept level, forming a right angle between the chin and the front of the neck. These instructions apply to all the sitting postures. In this position abdominal breathing is facilitated, and the feeling is one of alertness and poise, conducive to poised awareness.

Royal figures in the statues of ancient Egypt sit with the calm dignity of the position we have described, which is practical for all meditators, except invalids having to lie on their backs. The fullest benefits to be derived from meditation are possible in this position, but the strong points of the cross-legged postures should be sampled by persons with the necessary flexibility.

If there is discomfort in the Easy Posture, which is the simplest of the cross-legged postures, then use the Egyptian Posture as just described, and sit cross-legged for short periods at other times of the day, so that you become accustomed to it. Watching television, reading, listening to records – suitable opportunities are easily found for a few minutes sitting in the traditional postures of meditation. There are also the special exercises, given below, which prepare the joints and limbs for the classic positions.

Easy Posture

This is the easiest of the cross-legged sitting postures. The ankles are crossed tailor's fashion and the knees are kept as low as possible without discomfort. Follow the same instructions about keeping the back straight and the head level, as given for the Egyptian Posture. The hands may be cupped in the lap or the back of the right wrist may be placed on the right knee and the back of the left wrist on the left knee in the traditional position described for Perfect Posture.

FIG. 2 *Easy Posture*

Eventually, when the knees almost touch the ground, you will feel ready to progress to Perfect Posture or Lotus Posture. Meanwhile, you should practise the preparatory exercises for these two positions.

Breathe evenly into the abdomen, and vary the crossing of the ankles, sometimes left over right and sometimes right over left.

When you can bring your knees down close to the floor, you may find that you can uncross the ankles and bring the knees down on the floor while keeping one foot in front of and in contact with the other. This is known as the Burmese Posture.

Japanese or Thunderbolt Posture

Some people find this a satisfactory alternative to the cross-legged postures. The knees are kept together on the mat, the back erect, and you sit on the inner edges of the heels. This is a traditional

FIG. 3 *Thunderbolt Posture*

sitting posture in Japan, and in Indian Yoga it is the starting position for many other postures. Its Sanskrit Yogic title is Vajrasana or Thunderbolt Posture.

The palm of the right hand may be placed on the right thigh and the palm of the left hand placed on the left thigh, or the hands may be cupped in the lap as already described. Breathe freely through the nostrils, into the abdomen. The knee joints and the ankle joints may protest at first. Comfort can be obtained by placing a cushion below the buttocks and between the ankles. Some Japanese meditators use a cushion to protect the ankles, and Westerners should not hesitate to do so.

Preparation for Perfect Posture

Sit on the floor with the legs extended and spread well apart. Fold the left leg and, grasping the ankle, draw the left foot in against the body so that the sole of the foot is against the inside of the right leg and the heel pulled in against the perineum, the soft flesh between the genitals and the anus. The left knee stays down on the floor, and the right leg remains fully extended. Place your hands one on top of the other in your lap or rest the back of the right wrist on the right knee and the back of the left wrist on the left knee.

Breathe freely into the abdomen and sit perfectly still with the back erect for at least one minute. Then repeat, drawing in the right foot and keeping the left leg extended. Rest a minute or two, then repeat the exercise, bending first the left leg and then the right.

This is a useful exercise in itself, strengthening the back, limbering the legs and the hips, and calming the nervous system.

Preparation for Lotus Posture

This requires more flexibility than the preceding preparatory exercise. Again sit on the floor with the legs extended and spread well apart. Bend the left leg and, by grasping the left ankle, draw the upturned left foot high up on the right thigh near the groin. Support the trunk by placing the palm of the left hand a little behind and to the side of the left hip and the palm of the right hand a little behind and to the side of the right hip. Keep the back erect, and sustain the posture without any movement for at least half a minute. The right leg remains extended and the left knee should be brought down as low as possible to the floor. Breathe freely into the abdomen.

Repeat, placing the right foot on the left thigh and keeping the left leg extended. Rest a minute or so, then repeat, bending first the left leg and then the right.

Perfect Posture

The Sanskrit name for this traditional pose is *Siddhasana.* *Siddhas* are 'perfected' Yogins.

Sit on the floor with the legs extended. Bend your left leg and, grasping the ankle, draw the heel in against the perineum, be-

FIG. 4 *Perfect Posture*

tween the genitals and the anus. The right leg is then bent and
the right foot pulled in so that the heel is against the pubic bone
and the outer edge of the foot is inserted in the fold between the
calf and the thigh of the left leg. Sit firmly on the sitting bones,
the thighs and the knees in contact with the mat. The head
and the neck are poised in line with the spine. Breathe freely
through the nostrils, down into the abdomen.

There is a tradition in Yoga of placing the hands in a certain
way. The back of the right wrist rests on the right knee and the
back of the left wrist rests on the left knee. The tips of each fore-
finger and thumb are brought together to make a rough circle.
The other three fingers of each hand are kept straight and
together. The alternative is to rest one hand on top of the other
in your lap in the way already described.

Vary the crossing of the legs – sometimes left over right, sometimes right over left.

If the ankles are crossed so that each foot is inserted between the thigh and the calf of the opposite leg, the pose is called *Swastikasana* or Prosperous Posture.

Half-Lotus Posture

For the half-lotus only one foot is upturned on the opposite thigh. Before that, the other leg is bent and its foot brought in against either the perineum or the root of the opposite thigh. Both knees touch the mat. Keep the back poised and breathe freely through the nostrils.

Vary the crossing of the legs so that sometimes one foot is on the thigh and sometimes the other.

Lotus Posture

In Yoga, *Padmasana.* In the full lotus posture the right foot is upturned on the left thigh and the left foot is upturned on the

FIG. 5 *Lotus Posture*

right thigh. Both knees should touch the mat. The abdomen is relaxed, so that abdominal breathing comes naturally. You can either place the wrists on the knees in the traditional Yogic manner as described for Perfect Posture or let them lie, one on top of the other, in the lap. The back, as always in these poses of meditation, is erect and the head is poised easily so that you look straight ahead: the ears should be in line with the shoulders and the tip of the nose in line with the navel.

Well performed, with both knees touching the mat, this is a sitting pose of classic symmetry and of remarkable stability and self-containment. It is the pose which in the East is associated with the meditating Buddha. Many Westerners never achieve it – those that do will find it conducive to the right 'inner posture' for meditation.

Vary the crossing of the legs: right over left, left over right. This is a valuable exercise, promoting pelvic health and increasing flexibility in the legs and hips. The nervous system is toned and the spine strengthened.

POISED BREATHING

During meditation, always breathe through the nostrils, unless they are blocked. Breathe gently, but deeply, into the abdomen, so that the belly swells out slightly on each inhalation and draws back and flattens on each exhalation. As you breathe in, the large dome-shaped diaphragm descends and pushes out the abdomen; it rises on your breathing out and the abdomen flattens. You can become accustomed to the muscular action of abdominal breathing by placing the palms of the hands on the abdomen with the fingertips touching along the central line of the belly.

Thousands of years ago Eastern sages noticed the connection between respiration and states of mind. They saw how, when a person is agitated, or excited, his breathing becomes fast and jerky and, conversely, how when a person is calm and serene his breathing becomes slow, regular, quiet, and gentle. Teachers of meditation therefore instructed their pupils to breathe quietly, gently, smoothly and slowly at the start of meditation. Such breathing aids poised awareness, but it is an observable fact that as meditation deepens the breathing becomes slow, regular and quiet of its own accord. Tests on meditators show that during meditation oxygen consumption drops by as much as twenty per cent.

Whatever the method of meditation you employ, it will prove useful on first sitting down to observe your breathing in passive awareness for two or three minutes. Nothing calms the mind more quickly. The sensations of belly breathing, and the rising and falling of the muscles, themselves make a valuable focus for awareness in the meditation of 'mindfulness of breathing', which is described later in this book.

The Meditation Object

This may be something seen – a flower, a patch of blue sky, sunlight glinting on water, an icon, a special design for meditation (a *yantra*).

It may be something heard – the purling of a stream, the song of a bird, the ticking of a watch or a clock, the sound of silence.

It may be a feeling – religious adoration, loving attention.

It may be a word or a phrase that is repeated aloud or mentally.

It may be your own breath, coming into your body and going out in a constant process, or the slight swell and fall of the abdomen on inhalation and exhalation.

It is anything to which the attention can turn and on which it might rest for about twenty minutes, if you had the ability to sustain attention that long. Actually this does not happen. The attention is certain to wander – but the meditation object must always be there to come back to.

POISED AWARENESS

Attention and Awareness

In meditation, attention and awareness work together and form as essential a combination as lens and aperture are to the correct exposure of film to light. But the aperture is open all the time. Unless we are in dreamless sleep, awareness is ongoing. In meditation we point the lens at the meditation object and awareness receives it. The lens keeps shifting away from the meditation object – we patiently point it again in the right direction.

In Yoga meditation, the stage of *dharana* or concentration passes into *dhyana*, which is meditation or contemplation – attention then becomes effortless and pure awareness. The meditation object – a sight, a sound, a repeated word or a feeling – floats in the mind. When the attention wanders, it is effortlessly turned back to dwell once more upon the meditation object. Awareness is taken to deeper and deeper levels of consciousness and perception of the object becomes more and more subtle until finally the separations of subject and object, perceiver and perceived, are transcended. Then there is only pure consciousness. This is the stage which the Hindu Yogis and the Buddhists call *samadhi*.

The transition from concentration to *samadhi* is well brought out by Lama Anagarika Govinda in *The Way of the White Clouds* (Rider): 'The one-pointedness of our consciousness is similar to the focalisation of a lens; it can be utilised for bringing a particular object into focus, or for the focalisation of consciousness itself by excluding any particular object and just letting consciousness rest in itself, integrated in its own awareness. In such a state one is not holding on to anything or concentrating on anything; the mind is completely free from object-awareness or from the interference of will-power or intellectual activity.'

Passive Attitude to Distractions

Your attitude to distractions of all kinds should be passive. The attention is poised lightly on the meditation object. Inevitably it will wander. As soon as you are aware of the shift, gently, without fuss, bother, or irritation, bring attention back on to the object. Even if this has to be done many times, the return should always be gentle and unhurried.

Chögyam Trungpa, a Tibetan Buddhist in exile in the West, says of the attitude the meditator should take to distracting thoughts: 'Whenever thoughts arise, just observe them *as thoughts*, rather than as being a subject [that you become caught up in] . . . One should not try to suppress thoughts in meditation, but one should try to see the transitory nature, the translucent nature of thoughts. One should not become involved in them, nor reject them, but simply observe them and then come back to the

awareness of [the meditation object]. The whole point is to cultivate the acceptance of everything, and one should not discriminate or become involved in any kind of struggle. That is the basic
meditation technique, and it is quite simple and direct. There
should be no deliberate effort, no attempt to control and no
attempt to be peaceful.' (*Meditation in Action*, Stuart and
Watkins, London; Shambala Publications, Berkeley, California).

When Dr. Herbert Benson sought out the components of meditation that bring out the Relaxation Response, he came to the
view that 'a passive attitude' was the most important of them.

With practice, the return of the attention to the meditation
object becomes automatic and effortless. It is rather like being
carried down a smoothly flowing river by canoe. Now and again
the canoe moves off course and you have to dip the paddle into
the water to keep the canoe on course, poised and perfectly
balanced, at the very centre of the flow.

Psychic Phenomena

The passive attitude which has just been recommended for
coping with distracting thoughts and images applies equally to
those of a more showy, even startling, nature, which a small
number of meditators may experience at some time. Hallucina-
tions arise from prolonged sensory deprivation, but meditating
for up to thirty minutes is unlikely to produce them. In all the
major religions, visions, locutions, and various psychic phenomena that might arise in prolonged meditation are viewed as distractions, to be treated dispassionately and detachedly. They
should not become goals in themselves. In Zen, visions and
strange psychic activity are called *mayko* or 'diabolical phenomena'. The mystics of most religions warn against confusing
visions, locutions, and so on with genuine mystical experience,
which in its advanced stages is formless, wordless, and imageless.
St. Teresa of Avila had an emotional nature and saw visions;
but she acknowledged that at best they are signposts on the
mystical way. St. John of the Cross said 'not to seek visions, not
to be misled by them, and not to mistake them for the true
mystical union.' Genuine mystical experience is formless and
imageless. In Tibetan mysticism and in Tantric Yoga, visualisa-

tion is cultivated as a method of meditation, but that is a different matter because visualisation is under control and the images are eventually transcended.

Meditation releases tensions within the psyche. A meditator, as occasionally happens, who bursts into tears, should welcome the cathartic emotional release and any insight that accompanies it. Going out of the body is another experience for some meditators, especially those using the following breath method. It is unlikely to happen in meditations lasting about twenty minutes; but if it does, it should not be cause for alarm.

Meditation and Drugs

At no time should meditation and drugs be mixed. Meditative techniques have great power to alter consciousness, and reinforcement by powerful drugs could be dangerous. Meditation has proved a healthy alternative to the use of LSD and other drugs. Several studies have shown that meditation helps people give up the drug habit.

In one study made in 1969 at the University of California at Los Angeles, W. T. Windquist found that of 111 students who had regularly used psychedelic drugs, 86% stopped taking drugs and the remaining 14% took less shortly after starting Transcendental Meditation.

Dr. Herbert Benson and R. K. Wallace studied attitudes towards the use of drugs in 1,862 student teachers before and after learning Transcendental Meditation. It was found that the subjects progressively decreased their use of drugs as practice of meditation continued. A similar trend was found regarding the use of cigarettes and alcohol.

The Effortlessness of Meditation

Meditative awareness is effortless, smoothly flowing, poised, and purposeless at the time of meditating. If intention is present it is at subconscious levels and a result of the conscious effort required to sit down and meditate. It should not be consciously present *during* meditation. Desire for results as you meditate in fact robs you of results. The skater makes his initial thrust and then glides effortlessly over the ice, the skier moves down the snow-covered slope, the canoeist takes to the flowing river. Meditation is ruined if you keep thinking about meditation – what has to be done next? what is the experience like? how it is going? what are the results? ... these are fruitless questions. The most valuable stages of meditation are those in which there is pure awareness without thought. As soon as you start congratulating yourself: 'This is it!' it isn't! – As one Transcendental Meditator put it: 'You don't know you've been there until you get back.' Or as St. Teresa of Avila put it in the sixteenth century: 'The soul neither sees, hears nor understands while she is united to God – God establishes himself in the interior of the soul in such a way that when she comes to herself, it is impossible for her to doubt that she has been in God and God in her.'

Repeatedly directing attention to the meditation object releases the mind from its customary forms of linear thought and creates a channel, as it were, through which pure awareness flows effortlessly. In her autobiography, St. Teresa (1515–82) likened the degrees of prayer to four methods of watering a garden. Only the first two stages require directed attention – the third and fourth stages are those of effortless contemplation. The first stage she compares to drawing water by hand from a deep well; the second stage to the greater ease resulting from the use of a windlass; the third stage is like having a stream flowing through your garden; and the final stage she compares to rain falling on the garden.

St. Teresa was echoed by Maharishi Mahesh Logi in a television discussion programme which was transmitted by the BBC on 5 July 1964: 'We, in meditation, don't make an effort. We allow the mind to get into these more effortless [*sic*] states, because in experiencing the subtlest state of thought, effort is less and less, and less, and less, and then no effort, absolutely no effort.' (Quoted in Martin Ebon, ed. *Maharishi, The Guru: An International Symposium*, New American Library, New York).

Meditation as Non-Doing

Meditation is, paradoxically, a doing that is yet a non-doing,

or a non-doing that is yet a doing. It is letting go – yet fully
letting-go would result in sleep, not the alertly poised awareness
of meditation. Keeping trunk, spine, neck, and head in upright
line, insisted upon in most systems, is a way of preventing sleep
and maintaining poised wakefulness. Physical poise aids psychic
poise, outer posture aids inner posture. A passive attitude is a
passive posture. It might be interesting to read a few writers'
attempts to describe meditation.

'*Zazen* is the practice of the Buddha. *Zazen* is non-doing. This
is indeed the reality of the Self. Nothing else is to be sought after
in Buddhism.' Thus a Soto Zen text states that *zazen* or 'sitting
meditation' is the whole of Buddhism. Zen masters say that in
zazen you take aim without having a target.

'Meditation is sometimes referred to as "effortless concentration",' say the authors of *Growth Games* (Souvenir Press). 'The
fact that this seems paradoxical – how can you concentrate
without effort? – points up the difference between the meditative
experience and ordinary, wordy activity. Meditation is *non-*
doing. It is passivity combined with perception. It is as if you
departed from your body and turned off your thoughts and
became, instead, pure perception: a disembodied awareness.

'Non-doing requires effort of a negative sort, much like the
kind of exertion needed to relax a chronically tense muscle.'

Writers invariably resort to paradox in describing the nature
of meditative attention and awareness. Maharishi Mahesh Yogi's
slip of the tongue in speaking of 'more effortless states' of mind
is understandable. Monica Furlong tackles the same problem in
Contemplating Now (Hodder and Stoughton), an excellent little
book described as a 'Christian paperback', but worth reading by
everyone. 'Passivity is neither sleep nor lassitude,' she says, 'it is
what the Zen masters call a "purposeless tension". It is like the
surface tension of a pool of water, or the tension of a string on
an instrument which is not yet being played. It is flexible and
ready, reflecting as the pool reflects the sky.'

We can best slip out of the verbal contradictions that arise
when one attempts to describe the state of meditation with one of
those snappy conversational 'tricks' that the Zen masters employ
to enlighten their pupils.

'Master, how do I meditate?'

'You meditate.'

Actually the right inner posture is familiar to everyone, though you may not have used it much since childhood. Think back to moments in childhood when you sat still and listened to the sound of the rain or watching snowflakes floating lazily down. That is the passive awareness of meditation, without a thought in your head.

Regular Practice

With regular practice, the periods of pure thought-free awareness during meditation become more frequent and more prolonged. But you cannot force results – if you put on pressure you are no longer meditating. Here we go along with Goethe: 'Man errs as long as he strives' (*Faust, 1, Prolog im Himmel*), and with the Taoists, whose basic philosophy is non-striving (*wu wei*) and harmony with the Tao.

According to mystic tradition, in moments of pure awareness, in the gaps between thoughts, the meditator contacts the field of being. Meditation is 'letting being be', to borrow a phrase from Martin Heidegger.

Once the right level of awareness is found, poised and floating easily, progress is soon made. Practise daily, once or twice, for about twenty minutes each session. The experience is nearly always refreshing, relaxing, and peaceful – and, for some meditators, on occasions it triggers a peak experience, blissful, even ecstatic.

4

Awareness of Breathing:
Counting Breaths

BASIC TECHNIQUE

1. *Meditate in a place where distractions of noises, voices, and so on are within your tolerance level.*
2. *Sit motionless, poised, and comfortable.*
3. *Breathe quietly, gently, smoothly, and rhythmically. Breathe through the nostrils and down into the abdomen.*
4. *Let your attention dwell on your breathing, either being aware of the general in and out flow of breath or focusing on the tip of the nose, inside the nostrils, or in the abdomen a little below the navel. As your breathing should be abdominal, the lower abdomen makes an effective focus of awareness.*
5. *Count your breaths on exhalations from 'one' to 'ten', then start at 'one' again. On the first exhalation . . . 'one'; on the second exhalation . . . 'two'; on the third exhalation . . . 'three'; and so on. Following the tenth exhalation . . . 'ten', repeat the count of 'one' to 'ten' over ten exhalations. Continue in this way throughout the meditation.*
6. *Observe a relaxed and passive attitude towards distractions, including thoughts and images that flit in and out of the mind. Each time you become conscious that your attention has wandered away from counting breaths, become mindful of your breathing again and restart with; exhale . . . 'one'; exhale . . . 'two'; and so on. Do this as many times as is necessary, maintaining the relaxed and passive attitude.*

The preceding chapter described the basic conditions for the practice of sitting meditation. The most important of these are –

to use Buddhist-style language – Right Sitting, Right Breathing, and Right Awareness. All three elements must be present in formal meditation.

Right Breathing means *abdominal* breathing – abdominal breathing that is quiet, slow, smooth, and rhythmical. Harmonious is the single word that best sums it up. Normally, during meditation the inflow and outflow of air produces a sensation on the periphery of awareness at most. But in this chapter we will look at breathing as the focus of concentrative consciousness – as itself the *object* of meditation instead of its harmonious underlying accompaniment.

Among the various methods of meditation used in the East for calming the mind awareness of breathing is held in high esteem. It is practised by Hindus, Taoists, and Buddhists of several schools in India, Tibet, Japan, and across south-east Asia. In these traditions breathing meditation is associated not only with inducing peace of mind, but also with improving physical and mental health. It is also linked with techniques of spiritual healing. We find it again in Sufi practice, and as part of some forms of Christian contemplative prayer, in particular that of the Eastern Orthodox Church.

The Ideal Object of Meditation?

There are sound reasons why breathing makes an excellent object of meditation – some even say an *ideal* object of meditation. The reasons range from the practical to the profound.

Breathing meditation has been extensively praised for its effectiveness in producing all the benefits and goals of meditation mentioned in Chapters 1 and 2. These include more energy, better health, a stable nervous system, deep relaxation, tranquillity, clarity of mind, mastery over thought and feeling, improved concentration, psychic powers, spiritual strength, and mystical consciousness.

For many hundreds of years the Eastern psychological religions have recognised the importance of harmonious breathing for health and for relaxation and have put to practical use the interplay between the workings of respiration and states of consciousness discussed in the preceding chapter. When we are agitated and excited, we breathe rapidly, noisily, and jerkily. When we are relaxed and calm, we breathe slowly, silently, and smoothly. And at moments of crisis or great effort, we hold our breath. This relationship between respiration and the emotional life can be observed in ourselves and in others. Sages in the East observed the connection and saw that breathing could be regulated to aid meditation or become itself the object of meditation.

The method induces states of deep relaxation – the 'Relaxation Response' that Dr. Benson observed in his scientific studies of meditators. Breathing meditation relaxes body and mind. Awareness of breathing is perhaps the finest meditation for meditators whose main aim is psycho-physical relaxation. Pure awareness of quiet abdominal breathing calms and stabilises the nervous system and induces muscular and mental relaxation of remarkable depth and quality. It gives the impression of unravelling knots of tension in the musculature and of smoothing out crimps in consciousness. After a time, the meditator no longer feels 'I breathe' but rather 'I am breathed'. Then gradually the sense of 'I' fades until there is just 'breathing'. These are the right psychological conditions for letting go of the ego, which the mystical masters say is essential if the meditator is to Self-realise – that is, to realise the Self beyond the ego.

Breathing meditation is taught to beginners in most Eastern centres of spiritual training but it should not be thought of as a kind of mystics' five-finger exercise. Awareness of breathing is acknowledged as a method leading to the highest states of mystical consciousness, as well as to better health and deep relaxation.

There is, too, a very practical reason why breath makes an excellent object of meditation. It goes with us everywhere and is accessible for use at all times.

Breathing has the closest possible associations with being alive. We can survive for some days without food or water, but for only a few minutes without air. Though breathing continues involuntarily throughout life, its operation comes under both the involuntary and the voluntary nervous systems. We perforce must breathe and the involuntary nervous system sees to it that the lungs and other respiratory organs keep on taking in, processing, and expelling air. Yet we are given the ability to slow down, speed up, or suspend breathing when required: to sing, to swim under water, to avoid taking harmful fumes into the lungs, and so on. It is this ability to regulate the breath that the Yogis exploit for their ends.

Breath and Spirit

The esteem with which breathing meditation is held in the East is understandable in view of the association between breath and consciousness, healing, and spirit. In some Eastern languages the word for 'breath' is also the word for 'spirit'. The Sanskrit word *Atman*, the Self or Spirit in Man, originally meant 'breath'. The German word *atem* (breath) shares the same root. In several Eastern cultures breath is believed to be the mediator between matter and spirit and between body and spirit. But it was an English poet, Tennyson, who wrote: 'Closer is He than breath.' And when W. B. Yeats was asked how he composed a poem, he replied: 'Out of a mouthful of air.'

The inflow and outflow of air in breathing is associated in Indian and Chinese Yogas with positive and negative, masculine and feminine, energies in the universe. The Chinese call them *Yang* and *Yin*. Hindu Yogis have a concept of cosmic energy called *prana*. This force is said to be highly concentrated in air and can be converted into psychic or spiritual force within the body by combining controlled respiration and meditation. *Prana* is the power that heals a wound; and directed *prana* carries healing power.

The link between breathing and the cosmos contained in Chinese metaphysics is described by A. C. Graham in introducing the first chapter of his translation of *The Book of Lieh-tzu*, a classic of philosophical Taoism probably written about 300 AD. 'The cosmology of the *Lieh-tzu*, and of Chinese philosophy generally, assumes that *ch'i*, 'breath', 'air', is the basic material of the universe. The *ch'i* is constantly solidifying or dissolving; its substantiality is a matter of degree, one term of which is the absolute tenuity, the nothingness, of the Tao itself. The universe began with the condensation of the *ch'i* out of the void, the relatively light and pure *ch'i* rising to become heaven, the heavy and impure falling to become earth. Moving, opening-out, expanding, the *ch'i* is called Yang; returning to stillness, closing, contracting, it is called Yin. Between heaven and earth the Yang and Yin alternate like breathing out and in ("Is not the space between heaven and earth like a bellows?" *Tao Te Ching*, chapter 5) accounting for all pairs of opposites, movement and stillness, light and darkness, male and female, hardness and softness. Solid things are begotten by the active, rarefied, Yang breath of heaven, shaped by the passive, dense, Yin breath of earth, and in due course dissolve back into the nothingness from which they came. The human body is dense *ch'i* which has solidified and assumed shape, activated by the purer, free moving *ch'i* present inside it as breath and as the vital energies which circulate through the limbs.'

Lieh Tzu was said to have had the power of riding on the wind. When asked about this power, Lieh Tzu gave a philosophical rather than an occult explanation. 'I allowed my mind to think without restraint of whatever it pleased and my mouth to talk about what it pleased.' Such harmony with the course of life could produce the subjective feeling of floating on air. Breathing meditation – in advanced stages 'being breathed' rather than 'I breathe' – put the meditator into harmony with the flow of life, or the course of the Tao as the Chinese would say. Spiritual freedom is the goal of mysticism and in mystical literature the movement of air is a recurring symbol.

A Simple Practice

Beginners take to breathing meditation quickly and find the practice deeply satisfying. It has the great merit of simplicity.

You sit motionless in one of the postures described in the preceding chapter, remembering to keep your head, neck, and back in poised balance. Then you become passively aware of your breathing: the taking-in of air, the momentary pause, the release of stale air from the lungs and respiratory passages, another momentary pause, and the start of another breathing cycle. The beginning, middle, and end of an inhalation or exhalation should all remain continuously in awareness. If you find your attention has wandered, bring it back to the object of meditation and sustain once more a steady awareness. Wandering is inevitable and should be accepted in a relaxed way. After a little experience of meditating the attention switches back automatically and effortlessly to the breath.

Beginners are sometimes instructed to count the breaths from 'one' to 'ten' and then start at 'one' again. A count may be either on an inhalation or on an exhalation. Counting is an aid to concentration and prevents the attention from wandering.

Instructions vary when it comes to the best point on which to place the beam of attention. The whole process of inhaling and exhaling may become the focus of awareness, but usually a more specific body part is selected. The tip of the nose or the inside of the nostrils is favoured by some schools of meditation. However, the abdomen is the most popular focus of consciousness. If you breathe into the abdomen as taught in the preceding chapter there will be distinct sensations of movement around and below the navel and a point at the navel or a little below it holds the beam of attention.

The reader could not do better than to start breathing meditation now. Even if later you try out other methods – which require bringing passive awareness to objects other than the breath – awareness of breathing may still be used as an initial pacifier, quietening the mind and producing that 'inner posture' essential for effective meditation.

Broadly speaking, there are two ways of employing breathing meditation. The first way is by regulating the breath by conscious direction. The control is subtle, but control nevertheless. The second way is by applying meditative awareness to the act of breathing, without introducing any interference or conscious control. Actually, if bare attention is sustained for some minutes the rate and the quality of breathing will change slowly: respiration becomes slower, smoother, quieter, and more rhythmical. Regulation of the breath in meditation also aims at these changes, so that the results are the same in both methods. The way of bare passive awareness is the purer form of meditation. Buddhists call this 'mindfulness of breathing' and the method is said to have been used by the Buddha himself.

There is a further twofold approach. Firstly, breathing meditation may be used as a lead-in for another method. Secondly, it may be the sole method of meditation – a meditation in and for itself.

As an introduction or prelude to other forms of meditation, breathing awareness should be practised for five minutes or so. It will be found that it calms the nervous system, concentrates the attention, quietens thought, and opens up finer and deeper levels of consciousness.

YOGA BREATH CONTROLS

All the major schools of mysticism have recognised the importance of slow breathing in quietening the mind and of awareness of breathing as a meditation. The oldest of these mystical systems is Indian Yoga. It has the most extensive system of breath controls. From Indian Yoga we learn the importance of breathing for health and for meditation. The beneficial influence of rhythmical and harmonious breathing on health and on states of consciousness was observed and put into practice thousands of years ago by forest sages in India. In the classical *Upanishads*, which contain the teachings of the forest sages, there are references to the importance of awareness of breathing. And, as was shown in the preceding chapter, regulation of the breath is included in the eight limbs (*angas*) of the classic Royal Way or Raja Yoga systematised by Patanjali, known as the 'Father of Yoga'. The 'limbs' start with rules and observances for the moral life, go on to posture and breath control, and after that are concerned with the stages of meditation culminating in mystical consciousness (*samadhi*).

The system of Hatha Yoga, which is Tantric in origin, is based on breathing exercises. The word *Hatha* derives from two roots: *ha* meaning 'sun' and *tha* meaning 'moon'. The flow of air in the right nostril is called the 'sun breath' and the flow of breath in the left nostril is called the 'moon breath'. Yogic breath controls, called *pranayama,* aim at harmonising the positive (sun) and negative (moon) currents. In some of the breathing exercises of Hatha Yoga single nostrils are used alternately.

An adaptation of Hatha Yoga exercises is now practised by many thousands of men and women in Europe and in America, mainly in another of its major components – body postures. They afford an excellent way to gain and maintain suppleness, conservation of energy, and muscular relaxation. They also tone the nervous system and the glands. There is a concomitant calming influence on the mind.

For an account of the Yoga Postures and breath controls see my book *Yoga*, also in the Teach Yourself series.

Chinese Practice

Breathing meditation is closely associated with Chinese Taoist and Buddhist practice. Here again abdominal breathing is stressed. This is what Chuang Tzu, one of the three leading figures of philosophical Taoism, had in mind when he referred to the breath being 'in the heels'. Sitting on the heels – or more accurately the upturned soles of the feet – was the main meditative posture in Chuang Tzu's day, though later it was replaced by cross-legged sitting in the Indian manner.

In the writings of Chuang Tzu there is a description of *hsin chai* or 'fasting of the mind', which Thomas Merton, a Capuchin monk who wrote several books on Taoism and Zen, translates as follows:

> *Concentrate on the goal of meditation.*
> *Do not listen with your ear;*
> *Not with your mind but with your breath.*
> *Let hearing stop with your ear,*
> *Let the mind stop with its images.*
> *Breathing means to empty oneself and to wait for Tao.*
> *Tao abides only in the emptiness.*
> *This emptiness is the fasting mind.*

Chinese Yoga, like some forms of Indian Yoga, has used breath control exercises for the purposes of enhancing health and prolonging life. This approach is much in evidence in popular Taoism and was to be found among Chuang Tzu's contemporaries, for the sage was scathing about those who forgot the philosophy of the Tao in pursuit of physical well-being and longevity. 'Blowing and breathing with open mouth; inhaling and exhaling the breath; expelling the old breath and taking in new; passing their time like the dormant bear, stretching and twisting the neck like a bird – all this simply shows the desire for longevity. This is what the scholars who manipulate their breath, and the men who nourish the body and wish to live as long as P'eng Tsu, are fond of.' A similar criticism is heard today when persons interested primarily in the spiritual and mystical aspects of Yoga deplore the widespread practice of Yoga solely as a physical-culture.

Lu K'uan Yu's book *The Secrets of Chinese Meditation* shows the extent to which the Chinese have practised awareness of breathing both for better health and for mystical contemplation. This book gives accounts of methods of meditation as taught and practised by Taoists and Buddhists of the schools of Ch'an (Japanese, Zen), Pure Land, and T'ien T'ai (Japanese, Tendai). Awareness of breathing plays a prominent role in the meditation of each of the schools, either as the central technique or in preparing the way for other techniques of mind-stilling.

The T'ien T'ai teachings on meditation based on awareness of breathing are especially thorough and detailed. The school took its name from the T'ien T'ai Mountains, its original home. Lu K'uan Yu gives a translation of a description by a Chinese writer of the twentieth century of 'The Six Profound Dharma Doors' (*Lu Miao Fa Meng*) as taught by Master Chih 1, or Chih Che, at Wa Kuan monastery. Chih 1 was the Fourth Patriarch of the T'ien T'ai school. He died in 598 AD.

The Sanskrit word *dharma* (in Pali it is *dhamma*) has a variety of meanings, including 'law', 'doctrine', 'teaching', 'duty', 'truth', 'thing', and 'mental state'. Chih 1's method of meditation was based on progressively subtler awareness of the breath and contains the fundamental features of the practice of breathing meditation as taught in Buddhist schools: counting breaths, and following the breath. It is also worth quoting at length because we can here follow the process of effective meditation based on any form of sustained concentrative awareness, regardless of object. This process was described in the preceding chapter and was systematised by Patanjali in his famous *Yoga Sutras*. Effortless concentration leads to a harmonious balance between the meditator and the object of his meditation, in this case the breath. 'One-pointed' awareness is sustained steadily and smoothly until it slips into the stillness of contemplation. Contemplation deepens until the duality of subject (the meditator) and object (the breath) is transcended. Duality ends and the meditator knows his 'real nature' – his 'original face', as the Zenists say. This is a state of pure existence.

We give 'The Six Profound Dharma Doors', slightly edited, from *The Secrets of Chinese Meditation,* pp 160–2, by permission of the publishers, Rider and Co.

The Six Profound Dharma Doors centre on breath and are a thorough method of meditation . . . This method consists of (1) counting, (2) following, (3) stopping (*chih*), (4) contemplating (*kuan*), (5) returning and (6) purifying.

1. What is counting? This is the counting of breaths, of which there are two phases:

(a) *Practice by counting.* After a meditator has regulated his breath so that it is neither tight nor loose, he should count slowly, from one to ten, either his inhalation or exhalation, choosing whichever he likes, but on no account both. He should fix his attention on this counting so that his mind will not wander elsewhere. If before coming to the number ten, his mind suddenly thinks of something else, he should turn it back and start counting again from one. This is practice by counting.

(b) *Realisation by counting.* As time passes, the meditator becomes familiar with this counting from one to ten which will be orderly, until his breath is so fine that it becomes uncountable. This is realisation by counting.

2. Then he should stop counting and practise the method of following (the breath) of which there are two phases:

(a) *Practice by following (the breath).* After stopping to count his breath, he should concentrate his mind on following each inhalation and exhalation. Thus his mind will become at one with the ebb and flow of the breath.

(b) *Realisation by following (the breath).* As his mind gradually becomes refined and subtle, the meditator will notice the length of his breath, either long or short, and then will feel as if his breath passes through all the pores of his body. His intellect (or sixth consciousness) is now frozen, quiet and still. This is realisation by following the breath.

3. Gradually the meditator will notice that this method of following the breath is still coarse and should be given up and substituted with the practice of *chih* (stopping), of which there are two phases:

(a) *Practice of stopping* (*chih*). After ceasing to follow the breath, the meditator should, as if intentionally yet unintentionally, fix his mind on the tip of his nose. This is the practice of *chih* (stopping).

(b) *Realisation by stopping* (*chih*). In the course of this exercise, the meditator will suddenly perceive that his body and mind seem to vanish completely and he will thereby enter a state of stillness (*dhyana*). This is realisation by the practice of *chih*.

4. At this stage, the meditator should know that though the state of *dhyana* is good, he ought to turn back the light of his mind upon itself so that he can be clear about it and will not remain caught in this stillness. Thus he should practise contemplation of which there are two phases:

(a) *Practice by contemplation* (*kuan*). In this still state, he should look closely into his refined and subtle inhalations and exhalations which are like wind in the void and have no reality of their own. This is the practice of contemplation.

(b) *Realisation by contemplation* (*kuan*). As time passes, little by little, the eye of his mind will open and he will clearly feel as if his breath enters and leaves his body through all its pores. This is realisation by contemplation (*kuan*).

5. After a long practice of contemplation, it should be followed by the method of returning, of which there are two phases:

(a) *Practice of the returning method*. When the mind is set on contemplating the breath, there are created the subject, the mind that contemplates, and the object, the breath that is contemplated. These are the two extremes of a duality and are not an absolute state; they should, therefore, be returned to the fundamental mind. This is the practice of the returning method.

(b) Since this knower that contemplates (the breath) rises from the mind, it will also follow the mind in its fall. Since rise and fall are fundamentally illusory and unreal, the rising and falling mind is like water that rises in waves; waves are not the water whose fundamental face can be seen only after they have subsided. Therefore, the mind that rises and falls like waves is not the true self-mind. We should look into this true self-mind which is uncreated. As it is uncreated, it is beyond 'is' and is, therefore, void. Since it is void, it follows that there is no subjective mind that contemplates. Since there is no contemplating mind, it also follows that there is no object contemplated. Since knowledge and its object vanish, this is the realisation of the returning method.

6. After this realisation, there remains the idea of returning which should be wiped out by meditation on purity of which there are two phases:
(a) *Practice of the purifying method.* When the mind is pure and clean and ceases discriminating, this is the practice.
(b) *Realising the state of purity.* When the mind is still like calm water, with complete absence of false thinking, followed by the manifestation of the real mind which does not exist apart from this false thinking, the return of the false to the real is like subsiding waves that reveal water. This is the realisation of purity.

Three points arising from the above Chinese Buddhist method of breathing meditation are worthy of further attention and development. One is the practice of aiding concentration by counting breaths, a method much used in the Buddhist schools, where it is especially recommended for beginners. Note that this gives way to 'following the breath', our second noteworthy point. This is bare awareness of the breath, a technique known in Theravada Buddhism as 'mindfulness of breathing'. A third point worth taking up is the exact place on which to focus consciousness during meditation. In the description of The Six Dharma Doors the meditator is told to fix the attention on the tip of the nose. However, there are good reasons why the abdomen a little below the navel makes a better point of focus.

The first and the third points will receive development in the remaining pages of this chapter. First, we will discuss the method of counting breaths. Then we will see why the abdomen makes such an excellent focus for awareness. In Chapter 5 we will look at the second point, bare awareness ('mindfulness') of breathing.

Counting Breaths

In the meditation centres of the East beginners are usually instructed to 'count the breath'. After some weeks or months of practice they are told to drop the count and to 'follow the breath', which means to give bare attention to the breath. The two forms of meditation on breathing may also be performed successively, in which case the 'counting' always precedes the 'following'. Give the first five to ten minutes of a twenty-minute meditation to 'counting', then change to 'following'. Katsuki Sekida, in his manual on *Zen Training*, says that students should 'revert to counting the breaths from time to time, even though they have gone on to other kinds of exercises'. And he adds that when the experienced meditator returns to counting breaths, 'it leads to the development of an extraordinary brilliant condition of consciousness'.

The count is silent and inward. The usual method is to count either on an inhalation or on an exhalation, mostly on the latter. A breathing cycle of filling the lungs and emptying them represents 'one'. The count continues 'two', 'three', 'four', 'five', 'six', 'seven', 'eight', 'nine', and 'ten', by which time ten inhalations and exhalations will have been completed. You then return to a count of 'one' and continue up to 'ten' again, and so on.

Your breathing during the meditation should be of the type taught in the preceding chapter. This means breathing slowly, smoothly, silently and rhythmically deep into the belly; the belly inflates gently on each inhalation and pulls in on each exhalation. Such breathing relaxes body and mind, a beneficial effect deepened by focusing consciousness either in the nostrils where the flow of air can be felt or on the rising and falling of the belly.

The newcomer to meditation thinks that counting breaths up to 'ten' must be a simple practice, until he tries it and finds how soon and how often his attention keeps wandering. Between one count and the next a thought intrudes, or a whole train of thoughts. Or the trouble may be that some sound causes the attention to leap in its direction. Or an image forms before the mind's eye. Or a sequence of images start giving a film show on the screen of the mental cinema.

As soon as you become aware that the counting sequence has been broken, return immediately to the beginning – counting 'one', 'two', 'three', and so on. Here the instruction in the previous chapter about concentration being effortless must be observed. So it is never a matter of gritting the teeth or furrowing the brow and striving for a clear run without distraction to 'ten'. The competitive spirit does not enter into meditation. You should accept that interruptions of the flow of awareness are inevitable. You should therefore accept them lightly and gently return attention to the point of focus in the nostrils or in the belly and to the counting of breaths. By fixing awareness on a point in the body – the nostrils or the abdomen – you are aiding concentration and reducing markedly the number of times the attention wanders. The sitting posture, poised and immobile, itself provides support for the 'inner posture' that is steady awareness.

Some teachers of meditation tell their pupils to accompany the counting of breaths with some form of activity by the imagination. The following is one example. As you exhale and count 'one' silently, you think of the number 'one' as accompanying the breath on its path through the centre of the body until it rests securely in the pit of the stomach. As you inhale, you think of the 'one' as staying in the belly. On the following exhalation you place the 'two' on top of the 'one' or beside it in the abdomen, and so on until the 'ten' has been placed. You then mentally wipe out the ten numbers in the belly and start again with 'one'. This method aids concentration and focuses the attention below the navel on, according to Eastern tradition, the body's centre of gravity and chief source of spiritual and psychic strength.

Some Indian and Tibetan Yogis employ a similar technique of breathing meditation in which, instead of counting breaths, they visualise the sacred syllable OM and place it in the abdomen.

In Chinese practice the meditator is instructed to refine breathing to the point where he feels that the air is being inhaled and exhaled through every pore in the skin.

In Japan, Doctor Takemura found that neurotic patients benefited from practising the meditation of counting breaths. He measured the brain waves of the patients during breathing meditation and found that the customary Beta pattern that is characteristic of active brains gave way to the Alpha waves of relaxed brains at a level equivalent to that found in experienced practitioners of Zen meditation (*zazen*) in the early stages of meditation. The patients meditated in the Zen manner with eyes open, which makes the production of Alpha waves more difficult. Closing the eyes aids meditation and is advisable for all the methods taught in this book, with the exception of those that call for open-eyed gazing. Another interesting feature of Doctor Takemura's investigation was that his patients halved their normal rate of breathing and took six to nine breaths a minute. Such a marked slowing down would contribute to the 'Relaxation Response' and the deep psycho-physical relaxation must go a long way to explaining any therapeutic benefits.

The 'Centre' in the Belly

During breathing meditation the problem arises of the best place on which to focus the beam of attention. One way is to be aware of the total act of taking a breath, pausing, releasing the air, pausing again, taking another breath, and so on. This means that you are aware of the muscular movement of the act of breathing and also of the movement of air in the respiratory passages and in the lungs, both on filling the lungs and on emptying them. However, such a generalised awareness spreads the attention more broadly than is customary.

It is considered more effective to have a localised focus of attention. Such 'one-pointing' is likened in Eastern texts to tethering a monkey to a stake, and it helps to silence the 'monkey-chatter' of the mind.

Some old texts advise that the attention should be fixed between the eyes. We came across that in the Taoist method given above. In this writer's opinion, focusing attention between the eyes may cause eyestrain in inexperienced meditators. More acceptable during breathing meditation is to focus on the point where the flow of air is most noticeable. This is usually in the nostrils, either at the entrance or further back in the nose. Another point is at the back of the throat.

But there is an ancient Eastern tradition which favours the belly, at a point between five and eight centimetres (two to three inches) below the navel, as the most effective stake by which to tether the 'monkey-mind'.

The Japanese call this key 'centre' in the lower abdomen the *tanden*, and the influence of this concept extends from Zen to the practice of such sports as archery, judo, and sumo wrestling.

The Bamboo Method of Exhalation

Katsuki Sekida teaches a method of intermittent or wavelike exhalation during meditation as a way of strengthening the *tanden* and stopping thoughts. A long exhalation is either broken up by a series of pauses in breathing or the exhalation is continuous but repeatedly stressed by quick little 'pushes' centred in the abdomen. Both ways draw consciousness to the *tanden* and strengthen it. Mr. Sekida also employs the use of an inwardly voiced word or *mantra*, and we will return to this method in Chapter 11. It should be noted that as the meditation deepens what began as obvious conscious control slips into barely perceptible levels of breathing.

This method of breathing is not described elsewhere in Zen literature, though Mr. Sekida believes that 'many Zen students must have used this method without being aware of it'. A prolonged exhalation of this type should be followed each time by several breaths of normal length.

The name 'bamboo method of exhalation' derives from a similarity with the way a Japanese artist draws a bamboo trunk by intermittently lifting the brush from the paper to leave spaces representing the bamboo joints. A detailed account of the method is given in Katsuki Sekida's *Zen Training*.

'The Place of the Heart'

Before leaving this section on the significance of the belly as a focus of attention in meditation, we will look briefly at the presence of this practice in Christian spiritual training. It appears chiefly in the prayer and contemplation of the Eastern Orthodox Church. The monks of Mount Athos have a tradition of *omphaloskepsis* or concentration on the navel, combined with restraining the breath. Medieval instruction in 'Holy Prayer and Attention' is similar to the Zen Buddhist practice – described above – of 'looking into the *tanden*'. The centre of the belly is called 'the place of the heart' and it is said to be the root of the soul's powers. The similarities of concept and practice between Christian and Taoist and Buddhist contemplation becomes strikingly clear when we read the instructions on the Method of Holy Prayer and Attention attributed to Simeon the New Theologian. The two passages that follow are quoted by Jean Gouillard in his *Petite Philocalie de la prière du coeur* (Paris, 1953).

'Then seat yourself in a quiet cell, apart in a corner, and apply yourself to doing as I shall say. Close the door, raise your mind above any vain or transitory object. Then, pressing your beard against your chest, direct the eye of the body and with it all your mind upon the centre of your belly – this is, upon your navel – compress the inspiration of air passing through the nose so that you do not breathe easily, and mentally examine the interior of your entrails in search of the place of the heart, where all the powers of the soul delight to linger. In the beginning, you will find darkness and a stubborn opacity, but if you persevere, if you practise this exercise day and night, you will find – O wonder! – a boundless felicity.'

And again: 'As for you, as I have instructed you, sit down, compose your mind, introduce it – your mind, I say – into your nostrils; this is the road that the breath takes to reach the heart. Push it, force it to descend into your heart at the same time as the inhaled air. When it is there, you will see what joy will follow; you will have nothing to regret. As the man who returns home after an absence cannot contain his joy at again being with his wife and children, so the mind, when it is united with the soul, overflows with joy and ineffable delights. Therefore, my brother, accustom your mind not to hasten to depart from thence. At first, it has no zeal – that is the least that can be said – for this enclosure and confinement within. But once it has contracted the habit, it will find no more pleasure in wanderings without. For "the kingdom of God is within us" . . . '

The reference to 'pressing your beard against your chest' is interesting, for this is clearly the same method as the Chin Lock (*jalandhara bandha*) much used to restrain the breath in Indian Yoga. Pushing the breath down into the belly is also an instruction in esoteric Yoga. 'Direct the eye of the body and with it all your mind upon the centre of the belly' is the same instruction as the Zen master's 'look into the *tanden*'.

The extent, if any, of Eastern influence on Christianity has long been debated by the professors who have concerned themselves with such questions. These academic problems need not be raised here, but it may be mentioned in passing that the Eastern Orthodox Church has been in some ways a link between East and West.

5

Following the Breath
or Mindfulness of Breathing

1. *Meditate in a place where distractions of noises, voices, and so on are within your tolerance level.*
2. *Sit motionless, poised, and comfortable.*
3. *Breathe quietly, gently, smoothly, and rhythmically. Breathe through the nostrils and down into the abdomen.*
4. *Calmly follow the flow of your breath, without counting. Be aware of the in and out flow of breath in a general way, at the tip of the nose or in the nostrils, or of the swelling out of the abdomen and of its subsequent flattening and drawing in. There is an Oriental tradition which favours a point a little below the navel as the best place to focus awareness. Relax and let go, so that you feel you are being breathed rather than 'I breathe'.*
5. *Observe a relaxed and passive attitude towards distractions, including thoughts and images that flit in and out of the mind. Each time you become conscious that your attention has wandered, return patiently to bare awareness of breathing. Do this as many times as is necessary, maintaining the relaxed and passive attitude.*

After counting breaths for some weeks or months a sense of dissatisfaction usually arises and an urge to surrender to the breath itself without counting. The method of counting breaths described in the preceding chapter is an initial form of following the breath. But in following the breath proper there is no counting, no regulation of the breath, and breathing becomes the object of bare attention or what Buddhists of the Southern

School (Theravada) call 'mindfulness'. The flow of breath in and out is given full presence of mind.

Following the breath may occupy the whole of a formal sitting meditation, or complete a meditation that began with counting breaths, or begin a meditation that is completed by attention to a different object than the breath.

Practice

Sit motionless in one of the postures of meditation. This means sitting firmly and comfortably, keeping the back poised and the head level.

Keep your eyes gently closed.

Breathe naturally – that is, breathe *abdominally*. Allow the breath to follow its own rhythm. As the meditation deepens the breathing will become slow, smooth, and silent.

Rest the attention *effortlessly* on the abdomen and follow its rise during inhalation and its fall during exhalation. You should be aware too of the pause at the limit of each rise and fall of the abdomen as the breathing is about to change from an inbreath to an outbreath and from an outbreath to an inbreath.

Or focus attention in the nostrils where the flow of incoming and outgoing air can be felt.

Whichever of the above two points of focus for awareness is used, begin by resting the attention on it. Each time you become aware that the attention has wandered, return it gently to the point of focus in the abdomen a little below the navel, or in the nostrils. After some experience in meditation the attention is naturally attracted to the object of meditation and returns to it effortlessly. Distracting thoughts and images become less in time. They are inevitable for all but very experienced meditators and a neutral attitude should be taken towards them. Preserve a 'holy indifference' to their coming and going.

Allow the breath to flow without any attempt to control – not even regulation in the direction of smooth, silent, slow abdominal breathing. These results will come of themselves as the meditation deepens.

Surrender to the rhythm of breathing – to the rise and fall of the abdomen or to the inward or outward flow of air against the sensitive lining of the nostrils.

Though the main focus of attention is in the abdomen or in the nostrils, you will be aware of other sensations produced by the act of respiration. If your attention is in the abdomen then you are also aware, on the periphery of consciousness, of the air flowing in and out of the nostrils and brushing the sensitive mucous membrane, and also of the descent and ascent of the diaphragm and the poised opposition between diaphragm and abdomen at points when the breathing is momentarily suspended or when you almost stop breathing. There is also the expansion of the lower ribs in sympathy with the descent of the diaphragm in inhalation and the closing in of the thoracic cage during exhalation. If the main point of attention is in the nostrils, you will be aware, on the periphery of consciousness, of the rise and fall of the abdomen and of the movements and slight pressures of the diaphragm and the thoracic cage. In both cases there will be slight awareness too of the points of contact – the buttocks on the cushion and floor or chair seat and the hands on the knees or together in the lap. The skin too is a highly sensitive organ and you will be slightly aware on the edge of consciousness of its contact with clothing and air and of your surroundings in general.

It is worth saying again that the breathing should not be controlled in any way. Long breaths are allowed to be long breaths and short breaths are allowed to be short breaths. However, you should not be thinking 'This breath is long' or 'This breath is short'. There is no verbalising – only bare awareness. While you are meditating you should not think about the technique of meditating or of the reasons for your doing it. You 'watch' the breath without comment. 'Watch' here shall not be taken literally, but refers to sensory awareness. The eyes, as instructed above, are kept gently closed.

A strange discovery is made by the beginner in this meditation. It seems a simple practice just to sit and 'watch' the breath without interfering with its spontaneous rhythm and flow. But in early practice the meditator discovers that the mind is reluctant to let the body breathe without interfering. The mind is more accustomed either to controlling the breath or to being unconscious of it. For some minutes the novice usually finds that the breathing is uneven, sometimes almost stopping or stopping momentarily, then resuming with a jerk – and sometimes large quick breaths are taken that are not in harmony with the restful nature of meditation. But in time the breath gains its freedom and settles down to a constant slow, smooth, gentle, silent, and deep rhythm. In deep meditation the breathing rate slows down to a half or a third of the normal rate. As the movements of the abdomen – the ocean-like rise and fall – become more delicate and gentle, the influence of the meditation on consciousness becomes correspondingly more subtle and refining.

Alternative Methods

There are alternative methods of focusing the attention.

One may follow the breath so that awareness accompanies its entry into the nostrils and its slow deep journey deep into the body and then the return movement through the respiratory passages on exhalation – from the tip of the nose to the belly and then from the belly to the tip of the nose.

Some meditators find it helpful to visualise a kind of cloud of energy and light a few centimetres in front of the forehead. The meditator draws richly on this source of energy and light with each inhalation and visualises its inner journey deep down to the belly. The light and energy (*prana* or *chi*) are fully absorbed during the exhalation and the source before the forehead is drawn on again for the next inhalation.

Another useful visualisation, occasionally used in the Zen tradition, is to imagine a ball of lead descending through the centre of the body on each outbreath. The ball drops slowly and deeply so that the stale air from the lungs seems to fall out of the body rather than be squeezed out. For a description of the method, as described by Alan Watts in *The Way of Zen*, see page 74.

On the other hand, one may allow awareness to be free-floating, finding its own resting places. This method suits the 'open' style of meditation favoured in some schools.

Dealing With Distractions

During this meditation you should not have thoughts about breathing or about the results you hope to obtain from awareness of breathing. Let the attention be steady and let it be pure – that is, free of thought and imagery, unless you are consciously using one of the visualisation methods described above. This is too much to expect entirely, especially in early practice. The attention will certainly at times be drawn away from the abdomen or from the nostrils to fasten on such distractions as external sounds, or sensations on the skin or within the body. Thoughts, often of a surprising nature, will mysteriously arise in consciousness, and trigger associated thoughts. Images may intrude before the mind's eye, singly or linked in a moving-picture narrative. But each time you should gently and patiently bring attention back to the abdomen or to the nostrils. Be quite prepared to do this again and again. It is a matter of 'remembering' to do it – an act which the Theravada Buddhists call mindfulness or recollection.

Teachers in the Theravada Buddhist meditation centres of south-east Asia, where mindfulness of breathing is much taught, instruct beginners to use the following method of dealing with distractions. In this method the distractions themselves are used momentarily as objects of meditation, and mentally named. Thus a sound is mentally noted as 'sound', an itch as 'itch', a pain as 'pain', a thought as 'thought', an image as 'image', a feeling as 'feeling', and so on. The distraction is dissolved in the light of awareness. If a distraction is persistent, attention should be focused on it for several seconds. It is an example of the gentle art (Japanese, *judo*) of going with an opponent in order to overthrow him.

The Buddhism of the Southern School (Theravada) is much concerned with analysis, and there is a point to naming the distractions as they arise that is useful for that particular approach to enlightenment. You thereby gain insight into the contents of the mind. Unless attracted to this form of Buddhism it is probably best to simply return attention to the main point of focus after each interruption to the stream of awareness. This becomes effortless for the experienced meditator.

Another technique for coping with interruptions during meditation that is taught in Burma, Thailand, and other Theravada countries is 'touch consciousness'. This is to be employed when the attention is repeatedly wayward. For a minute or two the beam of awareness roams over all points of touch contact: buttocks on cushion, floor, or chair, hand on knees or hand on hand, and so on. Go over the points of contact a few times in sequence and then return to the main practice.

'Just Mindful'

The preceding description of how to follow the breath is based mainly on the Theravada Buddhist practice of 'mindfulness of breathing'. Mindfulness is said to have been practised and taught by the Buddha himself and is described in the *Satipatthana Sutta,* also known as the *'Discourse on the Practice of Mindfulness'*, an important text of the Pali canon. Nolan Pliny Jacobson, in his book *Buddhism: The Religion of Analysis*, says: 'What distinguishes the Theravada tradition from others is the complete seriousness with which it has taken the teachings in the Pali Canon regarding Satipatthana and the diligence with which it has provided conditions for its practice.' Mindfulness is at the heart of Theravada meditation.

The Buddha's *Satipatthana Sutta* opens and closes with the following words: 'There is one way, monks, for the purification of beings, for the overcoming of sorrows and grief, for the going down of sufferings and miseries, for winning the right path, for realising nibbana, that is to say, the four applications of mindfulness.' The four applications of mindfulness are: (i) awareness of the body; (ii) awareness of the feelings; (iii) awareness of states of mind; (iv) awareness of the contents of the mind. Awareness of the body begins with mindfulness of breathing.

The section on mindfulness of breathing in the *Satipatthana Sutta* opens with this succinct description of the practice: 'Herein, monks, a monk having gone to the forest, to the foot of a tree, or to an empty place, sits down cross-legged, keeps his body erect and his mindfulness alert. Just mindful he breathes in and mindful he breathes out.'

Here we have the essence of the Eastern contemplative technique – passive awareness combined with alertness.

Elsewhere in the Pali canon we find: 'This concentration of mind achieved through mindfulness of breathing, if cultivated and regularly practised, is peaceful and sublime, an unalloyed and happy state of mind that makes evil, unsalutary ideas immediately cease and vanish whenever they arise.'

The practice of mindfulness falls into two categories: general and main. General practice means bringing mindfulness or bare awareness to the morning ablutions, to brushing the teeth, to combing the hair, to dressing, to emptying the bladder, to eating, to drinking, to walking – in fact, to all daily activities. This application of contemplative awareness to everyday living will be returned to in a later chapter. Here and now we are concerned with the second category of Satipatthana practice. Main practice occurs in formal sitting meditation and consists of awareness of breathing, usually with the focus of attention on the rise and fall of the abdomen. You concentrate effortlessly on the involuntary abdominal movements: the rise on breathing in and the fall on breathing out. Whenever you become conscious that the attention has strayed, bring it back gently and patiently to the abdomen. The feeling tone of mindfulness of breathing is natural and unforced.

Full Awareness of the Here and Now

Satipatthana is most often translated as 'mindfulness', but 'awareness' is more direct. Another translation is 'recollection'. Bhikkhu Mangalo, in a concise, clear, and practical booklet entitled *A Manual of the Practice of Recollection* (The Buddhist Society, London), calls recollection 'quite simply, remembering to establish the attention with full awareness on the present, on the here and now.' The Buddha taught that mindfulness is to 'see clearly on the spot that object which is *now*, while finding and living in a still, unmoving state of mind.

Bhikkhu Mangalo says that *remembering* to give full attention to the here and now is recollection, and that 'the best way to start the practice of Recollection is, as the Buddha clearly describes in the *Satipatthana Sutta*, to sit down and establish the attention on the one most visible constant function of the body – the breathing. This is a semi-automatic function (*sankhara*) that is always present with us in normal life, and which is emotionally quite neutral. For these reasons it is the ideal object of use for learning to become recollected, and to hold one's attention on what is going on *now*, in the present, and *here*, in us.'

Bhikkhu Mangalo has reassuring words for anyone not comfortable in cross-legged sitting – 'nowadays even many meditation instructors in the East do their meditation sitting in a chair.' What is essential is that one should sit motionless in 'an alert, upright, perfectly straight-backed posture'.

This Buddhist teacher is one of those who recommend that the focus of attention should be 'at the face wherever it is most prominent'. This varies slightly from person to person. Some find the best spot to be just above the upper lip, others just at the tip of the nose, others again on the inside of the nostrils. It is immaterial. What is important is that it should be wherever one, oneself, finds it most clear. A few experimental breaths should soon establish that. The attention should be on the *physical sensation* of the touch of the air, not the *concept* of breathing. Nor should the breathing be interfered with or deliberately regulated. At first, this may be a little difficult, and in the preliminary stages it is not easy to dissociate *pure attention* from *control*. However, in that case one should just try to avoid unnecessary and unnatural control of the breath in any way, and just breathe easily, naturally and at a normal rhythm, but with the mind held on the sensation of the touch of the air. At first, too, it may well be found difficult to catch this touch of air clearly. Press on regardless. Practice and persistence will greatly improve this. One should try, moreover, to be aware of the sensation of the breath from the time it starts the inbreath until it stops, and then, again, from the start of the outbreath to its end. As one breathes in one should repeat "In", and as one breathes out one should repeat "Out". This is a check to see that the mind is really doing the practice and not wandering.'

The above passage reinforces several features of our instruction on breathing meditation – in particular the avoidance of effort or control. The inwardly repeated words 'In' and 'Out' aid concentration in a similar way to counting breaths and may be dropped later. However, the use of a word or *mantra* voiced mentally on either an inhalation or an exhalation makes for very effective meditation and this matter will be brought up again in Chapter 10.

An Experiment in Mindfulness

Admiral E. H. Shattock, in *An Experiment in Mindfulness* (Rider), gave a clear and unpretentious account of what constitutes training in *Satipatthana Sutta* – or 'the Burmese method' as it is sometimes called. A few years ago it was said that there were over two hundred meditation centres in Burma. There are also many meditation centres in Thailand. Lay persons join the centres for short courses in meditation. The British admiral reported his experiences of a course in *Satipatthana Sutta* in the Thathana Yeiktha at Rangoon. Though 'possessing no particular psychic qualities or leanings towards mysticism', he saw the possible value of Buddhist meditation as relaxation for a Westerner. Writing twenty years ago, before the physiological effects of meditation had been investigated in a scientific and thorough way, Admiral Shattock correctly observed: 'True meditation is relaxation, the deeper and more "formless" it is, the greater is the recuperative effect on the whole human system.'

When *An Experiment in Mindfulness* was published in the nineteen-fifties it was still unusual and somewhat novel for a European to practise meditation in an Eastern centre; by the sixties such training was almost commonplace; by the seventies meditation centres and teachers were available in many cities in Europe and America, and many books had been written by Europeans and Americans who learned meditation in India, Japan, Burma, Thailand, and other Eastern countries.

The method of training described by E. H. Shattock is basically what it is today. He had to give up all reading and writing and reduce his sleep to four hours nightly. The main practice, then as now, was alternating periods of breathing meditation and walking meditation, or, as the Buddhists of the Southern School say, mindfulness of breathing and mindfulness of walking. The walking stimulates the circulation and stretches the limbs after the formal sitting. Walking, like the breathing, is performed with contemplative awareness, and the alternation of these two activities continues throughout most of the day. Each period of walking or sitting meditation lasts about thirty minutes. The result is a great conservation of energy and calming of the nervous system so that four hours' sleep nightly is sufficient for the meditator. Passive contemplative awareness refreshes body and mind.

Walking usually takes place in a garden or on a veranda outside the meditator's room. The three phases of walking are followed mindfully: lifting the foot, swinging or pushing it forward, and placing the foot on the ground. The meditator is instructed mentally to name each movement. This may be 'up', 'forward', 'down' or 'lifting', 'swinging', 'placing' or any other choice of suitable words for the action of each foot. Walking should be slow to give time to distinguish and name the three phases. There are two additional acts, which again are noted and named – 'stopping' and 'turning'. Usually not more than fifty paces are taken before turning. The exercise may be performed in a room if outside space is not available. Walking that is both exercise and meditation is also a feature of the training routine at Zen Buddhist monasteries in Japan. The Buddha, in the *Satipatthana Sutta*, said that the mind can be purified from obstructing thoughts 'while walking up and down or sitting'.

The use of mindfulness of walking is valuable in intensive meditation that continues for several hours. It need not be linked with the sitting meditation that is performed once or twice a day. Mindfulness of walking is a rewarding practice and can be recommended to any person interested in developing mindfulness and in heightening awareness during everyday activity.

In dealing with distractions, Admiral Shattock was taught the customary technique of mentally noting an interruption and naming it – 'imagining', 'remembering', 'planning', or just 'wandering', and so on. This gives knowledge of the recurring contents of the mind and gives detachment from them. A persistent distraction was to receive the full light of awareness until 'its force had been expended'. This technique is taught by Bhikkhu Mangalo and other writers on Theravada meditation.

Mindfulness of breathing is used by Buddhists of the Southern School both for tranquillity meditation (*samatha-bhavana*) and for insight meditation (*vipassana-bhavana*). Stopping thought through pure awareness creates the right conditions for insight. 'Illumination is suddenly won as a result of all the efforts to deserialise thinking,' wrote E. H. Shattock, who was well pleased with his short experiment in mindfulness. 'The stream of thought has been broken, and a gap has occurred which has allowed the intuitional awareness of truth to break through.'

Being Breathed

It is in the Buddhist tradition that one finds the fullest development of the practice of bare awareness of breathing – so that the meditator feels that he or she is 'being breathed'. After a time there is neither subject (the meditator) nor object (the breath) but just the process of breathing itself. This accords with Buddhist belief that there is no such entity as an 'I' or ego – and therefore no 'I' that breathes, but only *breathing*; similarly, there is no 'I' that sees, but only *seeing*; no 'I' that hears, but only *hearing*, and so on with the other senses.

'Being breathed' leads naturally to 'being lived' – and to the spontaneous non-volitional living which the Chinese call *wu wei*. This is action which is at the same time 'non-action', because it is not operating from an ego-centre.

The following of the rise and fall of the breath by passive awareness is a central feature of Tibetan Buddhist practice. One of the most helpful accounts of this meditation comes from a talk on 'Meditation' given by Chögyam Trungpa, a Tibetan Buddhist who directed the Samye-Ling Tibetan Centre on its establishment in 1967 in the highlands of Scotland. It is published in his collection of talks entitled *Meditation in Action* (Stuart and Watkins). He sees awareness of breathing as ideal practice of the form of meditation that is concerned with seeing 'what is' and in which 'the concept of *nowness* plays an important part'. He says: 'One has to become aware of the present moment through such means as concentrating on the breathing, a practice which has been developed in the Buddhist tradition. This is based on developing the knowledge of nowness, for each respiration is unique, it is an expression of *now*. Each breath is separate from the next and is fully seen and fully felt, not in any visualised form, nor simply as an aid to concentration, but it should be fully and properly dealt with. Just as a very hungry man, when he is eating, is not even conscious that he is eating food. He is so engrossed in the food that he completely identifies himself with what he is doing and almost becomes one with the taste and enjoyment of it. Similarly, with the breathing, the whole idea is to try and see through that very moment in time.'

This 'seeing through' is *prajna* or wisdom.

We quoted Chögyam Trungpa earlier in discussing the question of whether passive awareness is or is not concentration, and it was said that if the word 'concentration' is applied then it should be qualified by the adjective 'effortless'. This 'effortless concentration' is nowhere more obvious than in the practice of mindfulness of breathing. When Chögyam Trungpa speaks of 'concentrating on the breathing' in the passage quoted above, he is referring to 'effortless concentration' or 'passive awareness', as will be clear from what he says a little later in his talk:

'This meditation is not concerned with trying to develop concentration . . . You see, generally one cannot really concentrate. If one tries very hard to concentrate, then one needs the thought that is concentrating on the subject and also something which makes that accelerate further. Thus there are two processes involved and the second process is a kind of watchman, which makes sure that you are doing it properly. That part of it must be taken away, otherwise one ends up being more self-conscious and merely aware that one is concentrating, rather than actually being in a state of concentration. This becomes a vicious circle. Therefore one cannot develop concentration alone, without taking away the centralised watchfulness, the trying to be careful – which is the ego. So the Samatha practice, the awareness of breathing, is not concerned with concentrating on the breathing.'

Shortly afterwards Chögyam Trungpa says: 'And for the breathing itself it is not a matter of concentrating, as we have already said, but of trying to become one with the feeling of breath. At the beginning some effort is needed, but after practising for a while the awareness is simply kept on the verge of the movement of breath; it just follows is quite naturally and one is not trying particularly to bind the mind to breathing. One tries to feel the breath – outbreathing, inbreathing, outbreathing, inbreathing – and it usually happens that the outbreathing is longer than the inbreathing, which helps one to become aware of space and the expansion of breathing outwards.

'It is also very important to avoid becoming solemn and to avoid the feeling that one is taking part in some special ritual. One should feel quite natural and spontaneous and simply try to identify oneself with the breath. That is all there is to it, and there are no ideas or analysing involved. Whatever thoughts arise, just observe them *as thoughts* rather than as being a subject . . . One should not try to suppress thoughts in meditation, but one should just try to see the transitory nature, the translucent nature of thoughts. One should not become involved in them, nor reject them, but simply observe them and then come back to the awareness of breathing. The whole point is to cultivate the acceptance of everything, so one should not discriminate or become involved in any kind of struggle. That is the basic meditation technique and it is quite simple and direct. There should be no deliberate effort, no attempt to control and no attempt to be peaceful. That is why breathing is used. It is easy to feel the breathing, and one has no need to be self-conscious or to try to do anything. The breathing is simply available and one should just feel that . . . This is not classified as an advanced technique or a beginners' technique. It simply grows and develops naturally.'

One could go further than the Tibetan teacher and say that awareness of breathing is effortless even in the beginning. There is no 'trying' at any stage. Interruptions of the purity of awareness are accepted as part of the meditation. Through time the meditation deepens and for longer periods there is simply *breathing*, a rise and fall and flow that is spontaneous and inseparable from pure existence.

Sufic techniques of meditation have been concealed more than those of most mystical traditions, but it is clear from the literature of Sufism that there is a prominent place for regulation of the breath, rhythmical breathing, and following the breath. Once again breathing operates principally from the abdomen.

There is a part of Sufism that is concerned with the conscious transformation of subtle energies, in which correct use of breathing is the key practice. And passive awareness of breathing for the Sufi, as for the Buddhist, can lead to insight concerning one's true identity.

Reshad Feild described his experiences of 'a Sufi journey' and discipleship in a book called *The Last Barrier* (Turnstone Books). The teacher, Hamid, gave the following instructions on breathing meditation:

' "First make sure that your back is straight, and then simply watch the rise and fall of the breath. To be able to do this takes much practice, and few people are prepared to make the necessary effort. When you can just watch the breath you will begin to realise that we are tyrannised by thoughts that move us this way and that almost constantly; and although we do not like to face the truth, it becomes clear to us that we have little of permanence. But you are *not* your thoughts, any more than you are your emotions or your body. If you are not your thoughts, and yet you find it so difficult just to watch the breath and not be moved by these thoughts, then is there not something wrong?"

'He put more pressure on my hands as he asked this question until I looked up into his eyes. "Listen carefully," he said, "and remember this – until you have a permanent 'I' you will always be in danger of being led astray. When you learn to breathe in awareness, then there is a chance to come upon this inner being that is your real Self." '

The master Sufi then taught a method of following the breath that is sometimes called 'The Mother's Breath'.

' "Make sure your spine is straight, so that the vital fluids can pass easily up and down. Now, inhale to a count of seven, pause for one, and breathe out for a count of seven. Before breathing in to start the second cycle, pause once more on the out breath for a count of one. This is a very simple rhythmic count of 7–1–7–1–7. If you work hard the timing will soon become automatic. Now practise this rhythm with me."

'As I relaxed and surrendered to the rhythm I began to feel very light. Hamid was still holding my hands, and I could see the rise and fall of his abdomen as he breathed. Although the rhythm was strange, and rather difficult to follow in the beginning, something in me started slowly to awake – an observer who was able to watch all that was going on and yet was not identified with the rhythm itself.

' "Good," said Hamid. "Now trust a little more, relax and close your eyes, and just allow yourself to be breathed. Let go of all concepts – surrender to the rhythm that flows and pulsates throughout all life. This rhythm is called the law of seven, and by following it you establish yourself as part of the harmonious principles of life which wishes only to conceive perfection from within itself." '

'Watching the Breath' in Zen

Another expression for 'following the breath' or 'mindfulness of breathing' is 'watching the breath'. 'Watching' is not to be taken literally, but refers to sensory awareness of inbreathing and out-breathing. This may or may not be centred on a specific body part: sometimes awareness is free-floating and allowed to find its own points of contact like water exploring new ground.

Zen masters will instruct a pupil to 'watch the breath' or to 'let the body breathe'. Alan Watts, in *The Way of Zen* (Penguin Books), is worth reading on this:

'Whether Zen is practised through *za-zen* [sitting meditation] or *cha-no-yu* [Tea Ceremony] or *kendo* [swordmanship], great importance is attached to the way of breathing. Not only is breathing one of the two fundamental rhythms of the body; it is also the process in which control and spontaneity, voluntary and involuntary action, find their most obvious identity. Long before the origins of the Zen School, both Indian *yoga* and Chinese Taoism practised "watching the breath", with a view to *letting* – not forcing – it to become as slow and silent as possible. Physiologically and psychologically, the relationship between breathing and "insight" is not yet altogether clear. But if we look at man as process rather than entity, rhythm rather than structure, it is obvious that breathing is something which he does – and thus *is* – constantly. Therefore grasping air with the lungs goes hand-in-hand with grasping at life.

'So-called "normal" breathing is fitful and anxious. The air is always being held and not fully released, for the individual seems incapable of "letting" it run its full course through the lungs. He breathes compulsively rather than freely. The technique therefore begins by encouraging a full release of the breath

– easing it out as if the body were being emptied of air by a great leaden ball sinking through the chest and abdomen, and settling down into the ground. The returning in-breath is then allowed to follow as a simple reflex action. The air is not actively inhaled; it is just allowed to come – and then, when the lungs are comfortably filled, it is allowed to go out once more, the image of a leaden ball giving it the sense of "falling" out as distinct from being pushed out.

'One might go as far as to say that this way of breathing is Zen itself in its physiological aspect. Yet, as with every other aspect of Zen, it is hindered by striving for it, and for this reason beginners in the breathing technique often develop the peculiar anxiety of feeling unable to breathe unless keeping up a conscious control. But just as there is no need to try to be in accord with the Tao, to try to see, or to try to hear, so it must be remembered that the breath will always take care of itself. This is not a breathing "exercise" so much as a "watching and letting" of the breath, and it is always a serious mistake to undertake it in the spirit of a compulsive discipline to be "practised" with a goal in mind.'

The image of a leaden ball 'sinking through the chest and abdomen and settling down into the ground' is helpful in training a meditator in deep abdominal breathing and particularly in steady, smooth and effortless out-breathing. However, visualisation of this kind is not often found in Zen meditation and may be dropped as soon as spontaneous abdominal breathing has been established. Thereafter the image may be employed occasionally to check that your breathing is as it should be.

The outcome of 'letting' the body breathe – which does not mean *trying* to let go of the act of respiration – is that the meditator feels he is being breathed or that 'it breathes', in the impersonal sense that 'it rains' or 'it snows'; also the body feels as insubstantial as the air that seems to permeate its every cell and to be passing in and out through all the pores of the skin. Such feelings of insubstantiality, transparency, and what in Zen is called 'the falling off of the body' have given rise to Oriental legends of sages who rode the wind or floated from the ground.

If considerable space has been given to awareness of breathing, it is because the practice suits almost all meditators and has a natural and peaceful feeling to it that makes it perfect practice for beginners, and also because it is rewarding at several levels. All forms of breathing meditation are effective in inducing deep states of bodily and mental relaxation, buoyant well-being and serenity, and feelings of harmony and union with universal rhythms and the flow of life.

6

Visual Meditation

1. *Meditate in a place where distractions of noises, voices, and so on are within your tolerance level.*
2. *Sit motionless, poised, and comfortable.*
3. *Breathe quietly, gently, smoothly, and rhythmically. Breathe through the nostrils and down into the abdomen.*
4. *Gaze in a relaxed way at any object that provides a pleasant or neutral visual stimulus for the duration of meditation. After a few minutes close your eyes and view the 'after image' in your mind. The object may be alternately gazed upon with your eyes open and then visualised with your eyes closed. After some time the meditation may be entirely visualisation of a favourite object — a flower, a rock, a religious symbol, a mandala or yantra (special designs for contemplation), and so on. As meditation progresses, the visual image becomes more subtle and refined.*
5. *Observe a relaxed and passive attitude towards distractions, including thoughts and images that flit in and out of the mind. Each time you become conscious that your attention has wandered away from the object of meditation, return it gently. Do this as many times as is necessary, maintaining the relaxed and passive attitude.*

In discussing the nature of meditation we pointed out that it is essential to have an object on which to allow the attention to dwell and to provide a constant stimulus. And we went on to point out that meditative awareness should be passive and effortless. Any object in your immediate environment towards which the gaze can be directed and on which it can rest for ten minutes or more may be used for visual meditation. An object may also be visualised within the mind.

Visual meditation may thus be practised with the eyes open or with them shut, or by opening and shutting the eyes for alternate periods. When the eyes are closed the image appears within the mind – before the mind's eye, as we say. A meditation may commence by gazing upon some object with open eyes, but in the concluding stages the eyes are closed and the image reproduced inwardly. With practice, inner pictures can be detailed and colourful. As the image is sustained in gazing meditation, whether with open or closed eyes, the image floats effortlessly and in deep meditation seer and seen become one. In advanced practice the image is progressively refined: gross contemplation with form is succeeded by luminous contemplation with brightness and clear light and in the highest stage by subtle contemplation in which even the luminosity has been transcended in the experience of pure consciousness.

Looking At A Flower

Tibetan Yogis visualise scenes of remarkable complexity, featuring numerous objects – but a single object, or a single part of an object, makes for the most direct and easy meditation for the beginner. The object that supports visual meditation may be of any kind, but most people will prefer to select something that is pleasant to look at or which evokes a neutral response. A flower is a favourite target for the attention. It may be in a vase or pot indoors or growing in the earth outdoors. It should be about a metre in front of the eyes and level with them. You sit before it, breathing quietly, and allow your gaze to fall calmly upon the bloom and to rest there.

Optional Preliminary Practice

There is a form of Yogic concentration (Sanskrit *dharana*) in which the meditator exhausts all possible thoughts about the object of meditation, so that afterwards the pure object remains without associations. In the example of a flower, this would mean asking and answering every possible question about it. What is its name? What does it look like? What colour is it?

Do not simply say 'blue' or 'red' or 'yellow' – look closely and observe that there is in fact a variety of tints and subtle gradations of colour. What is the character of the flower? Each flower does have a distinct personality. What conditions best favour the flower's growth? How did it grow? Visualise the stages of growth through the days and weeks to its present fullness. What lies ahead for the flower? Does the flower have any musical or literary associations for you? If you happen to be contemplating a rose, there is 'Rose Marie' and the roses that are blooming in Picardy, and the presentation of the rose in Richard Strauss's *Der Rosenkavalier*. There is Rose Maylie (really Rose Fleming) in Charles Dickens's *Oliver Twist* and Rose Dartle in *David Copperfield*. There is the scene in Shakespeare's *Henry VI* where Warwick plucks a white rose while Suffolk plucks a red one, committing themselves to the Yorkist and Lancastrian causes respectively – the War of the Roses. There are the roses that grew in Paradise and were without thorns (Genesis iii, 18). There are the rival stories of the origin of the rose. Zillah, a Jewish maid of Bethlehem was unjustly accused of offences for which she was condemned to be burned alive. But the flames burned her accuser, Hamuel, whom she had refused to marry, and the brands around Zillah turned into red roses. In Islamic tradition, as Mohammed ascended to heaven, drops of sweat fell from his brow and became white roses on touching earth, and those that fell from Al Borak, the animal he rode, turned into yellow roses. Staying with the rose, the meditator might think of the Rosicrucian Brotherhood – the 'Meritorious Order of the Rosy Cross' . . . and so on.

To continue the catalogue of thoughts associated with the flower would be wearisome – for some readers that point will have been reached already. Some writers on Yoga obviously consider this form of preliminary concentration useful – Professor Ernest Wood, for example – but they are mostly Western authors and the method does not seem to be prominent in most Eastern schools of meditation. In *Yoga* (Teach Yourself), I used the example of an apple rather than a flower to illustrate the practice, but I have to confess to feeling that the technique is most useful at the first few meditations with any object and thereafter may become tiresome and mechanical. We have made it clear that meditation will not be effective when there is strain. The preliminary questioning may be an effort, though laziness should not prevent its being given a fair trial.

The method has some similarities to the stripping of the skins of the ego-self described in Chapter 8. Readers should use the method if they find it helpful and effortless. Concentration is a useful faculty in intellectual life, and this exercise develops it. But as an aid in visual meditation, it will serve some people more than others. The latter will take comfort from the assurance that this technique is in the nature of an optional preliminary.

Main Practice

The main stage of passive awareness comes when the flower or other object is looked at with relaxed gaze, which is sustained as far as possible without the intrusion of thoughts and other images, even those associated with the object. Distractions, as in the other forms of meditation, are inevitable – to be expected and accepted easily. Sitting quietly, collecting your energies and directing attention to the flower is also a form of *dharana*, and a purer form than that of the preceding exercise. You will find that wholly attending to the flower with bare attention will mean that questions about shape and colour could be answered in surprising detail *following* a few minutes of meditation. And the flower is known in a way that questioning analysis could not achieve. People say after visual meditation with pure awareness: 'I never really *looked* at a flower before!' The same applies to an apple, a leaf, a blade of grass, a pebble or a button. Whatever object is gazed upon has tremendous *presence*. It is seen in its 'is-ness' or 'suchness', as the Zen Buddhists say.

It is important not to strain or to stare; look *through* the eyes rather than stare *from* them. It is important, too, to relax the facial muscles, especially those around the eyes. Bring relaxed though alert attention to rest on the object of contemplation.

Each time the attention wanders, lead it gently back to the object.

Alternating Looking and Visualising

At the first sign of eye strain, close the eyes and keep them closed for two or three minutes. You may find that a picture of the object appears spontaneously against the lowered eyelids. After you become used to gazing comfortably with the eyes open at a flower or any other selected object, you can change to the alternative method in which the eyes stay open for two or three minutes, and are then closed for a similar period – the cycle continues until the full period allotted for meditation has been completed. During the periods when the eyelids are lowered you should try to hold an image of the object in your mind. The picture keeps slipping away, but that should be expected and accepted easily. Each time you become aware that thoughts or other images or any forms of distraction have supplanted the main image, simply darken the 'mental cinema' and bring the meditative image back on the screen. With experience, this happens automatically.

This alternating method leads to the ability to visualise an object for the whole of the meditation. No actual object will then be essential. However, this advanced practice should only be reached after some months of meditation with an actual object before your eyes.

Gazing at a Candle Flame

A candle flame viewed against a background of dense blackness is one of the easiest images to sustain before the mind's eye. Even beginners usually manage to do it for short periods. But it becomes easier if you practise for some weeks sitting before a lighted candle in a darkened room. Make sure the room is free from draughts – a steady flame on which to gaze is conducive to steadiness of mind. Your gaze should be as unwavering as the flame. On closing the eyes an after-image often appears. In a short time you should be able to hold a bright clear image of the flame before the mind's eye.

Hindu Yogis call this practice *trataka,* and they say that it purifies vision and perception. It is one of the six *kriyas* or 'cleansing duties'. Any alternative bright object may be used. A coloured fifteen watt bulb makes a substitute for the candle. Ramamurti Mishra, in *Fundamentals of Yoga* (Julian Press, New York, 1959), writes of 'tratakam on blue light' – focusing attention on an illuminated blue bulb of low voltage. An electric light bulb has not the significance of the flame, which acts as a symbol for both light and fire.

Following ancient traditions, Hindus and Buddhists base visual meditations on each of the elements – earth, water, fire, and air. In the practices of the Theravada school of Buddhism they are called *kasina* meditations.

Kasina Meditations

The *kasina* meditations have a long history and are described in the *Vissuddhimagga* or 'Path of Purity', compiled in the fourth century AD in Ceylon by Buddhaghosha, a Brahman converted to Buddhism. Buddhagosha was the first Buddhist commentator. The concise account that follows is based on the exposition by Paravahera Vajiranana Mahathera, who is a modern commentator on the Pali texts on which the Theravada school of Buddhism base their doctrines and practices, in his book *Buddhist Meditation in Theory and Practice* (M. D. Gunasena, Colombo). Professor Frederick Spiegelberg's *Spiritual Practices of India* (The Citadel Press, New York), has also proved helpful.

The *kasina*-device or object for visual meditation is hung on a wall at eye-level or placed on a low table or on the ground at a distance of about two metres from the seated meditator. The disc-shaped device should be about twenty-eight centimetres in diameter. These figures are approximate guides and need not be followed rigidly. Suitable objects *in situ* may also be used for meditation.

The *kasina*-device is gazed upon calmly with the eyes not fully opened. (I see nothing wrong with relaxed gazing with the eyes fully opened; some meditators find the half-open position tiring.) Then the eyes are closed gently and the image is viewed mentally. Opening and closing the eyes alternates' until the inner image – a copy of the original – is sustained clearly before the mind's eye. Eventually, for the experienced meditator, the inner image is 'spiritualised', that is, refined from gross to subtle. This 'spiritual image' – which Professor Spiegelberg calls the 'Counterpart' and Paravahera Vajiranana Mahathera the 'after-image' –

is free from the imperfections of the *kasina*-device as seen with opened or partly-opened eyes.

Kasina is a Pali word meaning 'entire' or 'whole'. The equivalent Sanskrit word is *krtsna*. The meaning of some other Pali terms should be noted. They refer to the process described in the preceding paragraph. *Nimitta* means 'a sign or mark'. The *parikamma-nimitta* is the object meditated upon. When it has been gazed upon for some time the eyes are then closed and a mental image floats before the mind's eye – 'an exact copy of the object, with all its original faults (*kasina-dosa*), presented to the mind as a vivid reality, as though it were actually seen by the eye,' says Paravahera Vajiranana Mahathera. 'This image is termed *uggaha-nimitta* . . . the "sign to be grasped", "the mark for upholding", or "the mark of upholding".' As the meditation deepens the image in the mind progressively refines. 'This primary concentration divests the image of its limited or moulded form, colour and shape . . . and turns it into a concept or abstract idea which is yet individual, since it is connected with a particular object. This conceptualised image is termed "*patibhaga-nimitta*", the "after-image", which is no longer presented to the senses or to the cognitive faculties as a concrete object. But this image remains in the mind as an emblematic representation of the whole quality or element that it symbolises.'

Ten separate *kasina*-devices are used for visual meditation, aiming at the transformation of consciousness that is associated with Buddhist *jhana* (Sanskrit, *dhyana*), meaning 'meditation' or 'contemplation'. They are the four elements earth, water, fire, and air; the four colours blue, yellow, red, and white; and light and space. In addition to looking and visualising, meditators may repeat silently the name of the object meditated upon – 'earth', 'water', and so on.

1. Earth-kasina

The visual attention of the meditator is directed to a disc of earth and rests there. Professor Spiegelberg, in *Spiritual Practices of India*, says that the device should be composed of light brown loam and spread 'with a perfectly smooth stone into a round level disc'. He continues: 'The loam that is used for this purpose must be thoroughly kneaded, and all grass, roots, sand, and gravel removed from it . . . The Kasina disc must not be so far away that it cannot be perceived distinctly; but at the same time it must not be so close that the unavoidable little unevennesses of its surface are visible . . .

'The aim now is to evolve the "spiritual image" of the Kasina disc. To do this [he] must contemplate the disc continuously over a long period of time, seated in an attitude of serene, motionless concentration . . . His eyes should be kept only partly open, and he should gaze at the disc in a calm, relaxed manner, somewhat as though he were looking at his face in a mirror . . . After a while he may begin to open and close his eyes, for a hundred times or a thousand, until the spiritual image of the disc rises within him. This image will then appear to him just as distinctly when his eyes are closed as when they are open.

'At this point [he] may experiment by leaving the place of meditation for a little while in order to see whether the image will remain fixed within him even when he is in another place. If it does not remain he must return and resume his contemplation. Through this exercise he finally succeeds in unfolding the "Counterpart", which exists entirely within him, and in which, consequently, there no longer appear any of the imperfections of the disc that is being meditated on. It is free from earth and all other material attributes, and is pure and luminous as the disc of the moon . . .

'The point of primary importance is that he should really create such a meditation-image to accompany him continuously; only as a secondary consideration does it matter what this particular image may be, that is, through which one of the Kasina exercises it has been produced.'

A ploughed field in the distance, a freshly-raked garden border a few feet away, or the soil in a flower pot that is placed quite close before you as you sit in a room . . . any of these will serve as earth-*kasinas*.

The instruction given above for creating a meditation-image within the mind that will be available at all times may be applied to any of the remaining nine *kasina*-devices.

2. *Water-kasina*

A bowl filled with water, preferably filled with rain water or water drawn from a stream, river, pond, lake, sea. Paravahera Vajiranana Mahathera says: 'If there is movement in the water or bubbles are present the same features may appear in the *uggaha-nimitta* [the copy image]. The *patibhaga-nimitta* [after-image], however, will be motionless, and like a jewelled fan or a mirror placed in the sky.'

3. *Fire-kasina*

A candle flame. The flame of a fire or a lamp or a cooking stove. The sun.

Paravahera Vajiranana Mahathera says: 'When a disciple obtains the *nimitta* in an ordinary fire, that is, in one not prepared for this purpose, the defect of the device may also appear, whether it be a piece of burnt wood, a burning coal, ash or smoke. When it is once developed into the *patibhaga-nimitta* or "after-image", it appears like a piece of red blanket, a golden fan or pillar placed in the sky.'

4. *Air-kasina*

You cannot see the wind directly, but you can gaze upon something moved by the wind. A tree-top; a flag; a kite; clouds; the surface of water; a rush; a blade of grass; a feather; a piece of fleece; a handkerchief on a clothes-line; a curtain. Try to observe the wind at its point of contact with that which it moves. Buddhist meditators say that copy-images and after-images are attainable. Paravahera Vajiranana Mahathera writes: 'In this meditation the *uggaha-nimitta* appears shaky, something like a ring of steam rising from rice gruel when just taken out of the oven. But the after-image is steady and well-defined.'

5. *Blue-kasina*

Anything blue. Blue flower or flowers; blue cloth; blue metal; blue stone; blue paint; blue sky; blue sea; blue lake; blue hills or mountains, and so on. Some Buddhist meditators use a specially prepared blue disc which is fixed to a wall. Objects may be framed and hung or set up for meditation.

Paravahera Vajiranana Mahathera says that the beginner 'should take a bunch of (blue) flowers . . . and arrange them in a basket or upon a round tray, so that they may assume the form of a round, dense, blue object, care being taken that no pollen or stalks may be seen.' The copy-image has the 'faults' of the original symbol: the markings and variations in the colouring. 'But the "after-image" appears free from all these, pure and clear like a fan made from a blue jewel.'

6. *Yellow-kasina*

Anything yellow. A yellow flower; yellow leaf; yellow straw; yellow corn; yellow cloth; yellow paint; yellow paper; yellow toy, and so on.

Practise the meditation on similar lines to those indicated above for the blue-*kasina*. The after-image in these colour *kasinas* is of great purity and beauty.

7. *Red-kasina*

Anything red. A red flower (such as a rose or a poppy); red earth; red sky; red cloth; red paint; illuminated red electric light-bulb; a streak of paint.

Practise the meditation as indicated for the blue-*kasina*.

8. *White-kasina*

Anything white. Snowdrop; snow; frost; white silk, cotton, linen; a white stone or pebble; chalk; white paper; the snowcap on a mountain; the crests of waves, a white disc and so on.

Meditate on similar lines to those indicated for the blue *kasina*.

9. *Light-kasina*

Light seen through a window; through foliage; through a hole in a wall; sunlight on water; a patch of sunlight or moonlight on a wall; the disc of light cast on a wall by a lamp or candle or a torch; a sunlit cloud; any bright object.

Here again the first image to appear before the mind's eye, after the eyes have been closed, is an exact copy of what was originally seen. But the 'after-image', the image following refinement through continued meditation, appears as 'a mass of bright illumination'.

Bright clear light is the chief symbol used by mystics to describe the experience of pure consciousness and of enlightenment.

10. *Space-kasina*

Window-space; a hole in a wall; an open doorway; the gap between buildings, mountains, trees; a keyhole; a night sky; empty bowl or cup; and so on.

The original image and the copy-image are limited, but the after-image 'appears without limits'. This is looking into the 'space of consciousness' (Sanskrit, *cidakasha*).

Worth pondering in relation to this space-*kasina* – though not during the actual meditation, for the *kasina* meditations are not occasions for thought – is Chapter 11 of Lao Tzu's *Tao Te Ching*:

> *Thirty spokes unite in one nave,*
> *And because of the part where nothing exists*
> *We have the use of a carriage wheel.*
> *Clay is moulded into vessels,*
> *And because of the space where nothing exists*
> *We are able to use them as vessels.*
> *Doors and windows are cut out in the walls of a house,*
> *And because they are empty spaces, we are able to use them.*
> *Therefore, on the one hand we have the benefit of existence,*
> *And on the other, we make use of non-existence.*
>
> (translated Ch'u Ta-kao)

Significant Symbols

The *kasina*-devices are symbols. Those representing earth, water, fire, and air have elemental force. Those representing light and space expand consciousness. Those representing colours set up vibrations within the psyche that influence consciousness.

Depth and resonance may be added to visual meditation by choosing a significant symbol as the focus for attention. It is true that *any* constant visual stimulus can be effective for visual meditation, as long as the other essential conditions are present – poised posture, poised breathing, and poised awareness. But significant forms – significant, that is, to the meditator – have a potency that is helpful in alerting awareness and in establishing a vibrant tone for the meditation. There is, too, such a thing as significant form in the abstract which evokes a deep inner response. Suzanne Langer has written eruditely on this matter.

Artists, if they are skilled, make use of this significant visual form, purely in abstract painting and inherently in representational painting. It can also be discovered fortuitously in Nature – we are 'captured' and held by the shape of a tree, a flower, a rock, a hill, and so on. Artists have a special genius for finding significant forms in Nature. Mystics, who have an even more special genius, see it all around them wherever they go.

Symbols should not be confused with signs, which have little or no resonance. Signs denote the object they represent and nothing more. They convey precise information by abbreviation. Concisely, they say what they have to say and no more than that. Signs have clear-cut meanings. Symbols imply an immeasurable wealth of meaning beyond the literal interpretation of the symbol. If signs are prose, then symbols are poetry. A symbol has overtones that go on sounding long after we have been in contact with it. During visual meditation you do not think of the associations or of all the possible meanings – unless you are following the preliminary method described above in which all thinking is exhausted deliberately, before meditative awareness begins properly. Without pondering the significance of the symbol, its invisible aura of meaning is still potent and acts on the meditator's consciousness.

J. J. Bachofen, in *An Essay on Mortuary Symbolism*, cited by T. C. Stewart in his *The City As An Image Of Man* (Latimer Press), writes cogently of the beauty and power of the symbol: 'Human language is too feeble to convey all the thoughts aroused by the alternation of life and death and the sublime hopes of the initiate. Only the symbol awakens intimations; speech can only explain. The symbol plucks all the strings of the human spirit at once; speech is compelled to take up a single thought at a time. The symbol strikes its roots in the most secret depths of the soul; language skims over the surface of the understanding like a soft breeze. The symbol aims inward; language outward. Only the symbol can combine the most disparate elements into a unitary impression. Language deals in successive particulars; it expresses bit by bit what must be brought home to the soul at a single glance if it is to affect us profoundly. Words make the infinite finite, symbols carry the spirit beyond the finite world of becoming into the realm of infinite being.'

'Spiritual Senses'

Religious natures find certain objects and designs charged with the numinous – the combined feeling of attraction and awe characteristic of man's sense of communion with the Absolute or God. And because mystics are concerned with that which is beyond human understanding they employ symbolic language and images.

Mystics, in attempting to describe the ineffable nature of their experiences, resort to symbolic imagery which can at least 'point a finger at the moon', as they say in Zen. Most of them draw on the language of the senses in striving to give ordinary men and women some inkling of what mystical consciousness is like. It is as though the mystic has refined his senses and spiritualised them – which is what Yoga and similar systems of meditation are said to do. Maharishi Mahesh Yogi speaks of the restructuring of the nervous system that results from twice daily practice of transcendental meditation.

St. Augustine was remarkable in that he responded to God with all five 'spiritual senses' awake and active. In his *Confessions* (10, 6) he wrote:

'When I love You, what am I loving? Not the beauty of a physical body, not the attractiveness of the season, not the brilliance of a light which our eyes love so well, not the charming melodies of songs of all kinds, not the sweet fragrance of flowers or scents or spices, not manna or honey, not limbs asking for physical embrace: when I love my God, it is not these that I love. Yet I do love a kind of light, a kind of sound, a kind of scent, a kind of food, a kind of embrace, in loving my God, the light, sound, scent, food and embrace of my inner man, where a light shines in my soul which space cannot contain, a melody rings which time cannot snatch away, a scent breathes which no wind can scatter, there is a savour which eating does not diminish, and an embrace which is not broken by satiety. When I love my God, it is this that I am loving.'

But it is rare for a single mystic to make use of the language of all the senses. Usually one or two senses predominate, and most predominant of all is the language of sight. The supreme experience for the Christian or Islamic mystic is the Beatific Vision in which the Divine Essence is beheld in ecstasy. The Hindu Vedantist's communion with Brahman, the impersonal Absolute or universal consciousness, tends also to be described as a 'seeing', and it too is blissful: *Sat Cit Ananda* (Being-Awareness-Bliss).

Light is the most powerful universal symbol for mystical consciousness, en*light*enment, God or the Absolute.

'Sight and visibility is but one power of light,' wrote William Law (1686–1761), and he continues:

'but light is all power, it is life; and every joyful sensibility of life is from it. "In Him," says the Apostle, "was light, and the light was the life of men."

'Light is all things, and no thing. It is no thing because it is supernatural; it is all things because every good power and perfection of everything is from it. No joy or rejoicing in any creature but from the power and joy of light. No meekness, benevolence, or goodness, in angel, man, or any creature, but where light is the lord of its life. Life itself begins no sooner, rises no higher, has no other glory than as the light begins and leads it on. Sounds have no softness, flowers and gums have no sweetness, plants and fruits have no growth but as the mystery of light opens itself in them.

'Whatever is delightful and ravishing, sublime and glorious, in spirits, minds or bodies, either in Heaven or on earth, is from the power of supernatural light opening its endless wonders in them. Hell has no misery, horror, or distraction, but because it has no communication with the supernatural light. And did not the supernatural light stream forth its blessings into this world through the materiality of the sun, all outward nature would be full of the horror of hell.' (*The Spirit of Love*, ii, 26.)

The *Bhagavad Gita* X1, 12 compares the Supreme Spirit to 'the light of a thousand suns'. And here is how the *Mundaka Upanishad* speaks of universal consciousness or spirit: 'In a beautiful golden scabbard hides the stainless, indivisible, luminous Spirit.

'Neither sun, moon, star, neither fire nor lighting, lights Him. When he shines, everything begins to shine. Everything in the world reflects His light.'

The imagery of light irradiates the mystical literature of many cultures.

'God is light,' said Walter Hilton (d. 1396), the English mystic who wrote *The Scale of Perfection*. And Hildegarde of Bingen (1098–1179), a German Benedictine nun, said that God was '*Lux vivens*, living light'. The motif of brilliant points of light dominates the illustrations with which she accompanied her writings. She was a theologian, a scientist, a poet, an ecstatic, and a visionary. She said that her visions were 'beheld neither in sleep, nor in dream, nor in madness, nor with the eyes of the body, nor with physical ears, nor in hidden places, but wakeful, alert, with the eyes of the spirit and with inward ears . . . ' A recurring vision was of a blazing red light: 'From my infancy up to the present time, I now being more than seventy years of age, I have always seen this light, in my spirit and not with external eyes, nor with any thoughts of my heart, nor with help from my senses. But my outward eyes remain open and the other corporeal senses retain their activity. The light which I see is not located, but yet it is more brilliant than the sun, nor can I examine its height, length or breadth, and I name it "the cloud of the living light",' and she goes on, 'But sometimes I behold within this light another light which I name "the living light itself". And when I look upon it every sadness and pain vanishes from my memory, so that I am again as a simple maid and not as an old woman.' (These extracts are taken from Professor John Ferguson's *An Illustrated Encyclopedia of Mysticism and the Mystery Religions*, Thames and Hudson.)

Jakob Boehme (1575–1624), whose mysticism has similarities with that of the East, contemplated a spot of sunlight reflecting from his cobbler's crystal and thereafter, he said, whatever he looked upon radiated divine light.

Mystics report the experience of seeing bright light at moments of exaltation or insight, often accompanied by great heat. Fire is another prominent mystical symbol. When Blaise Pascal (1623–62) died, there was found stitched into his clothes a drawing of a fiery cross and his concise but intense account of a mystical experience:

In the year of grace 1654...
From about half-past ten in the evening to
about half an hour after midnight.
   FIRE.
God of Abraham, God of Isaac, God of Jacob,
Not the God of philosophers and scholars.
Absolute Certainty: Beyond reason. Joy. Peace.
Forgetfulness of the world and everything but God.
The world has not known thee, but I have known thee.
Joy! Joy! Joy! Tears of joy.

Yantras and Mandalas

Eastern artists produce special form-symbols called *yantras* and *mandalas* whose purpose is to provide significant foci for visual meditation. Their most intensive development and use has been in Indian and Tibetan Tantric Yoga. Tantric Yogis look on these visual symbols as mirror-devices which reflect the Self, and call them 'seeds' (Sanskrit, *bija*) because if they are planted in the mind they will grow and flower.

Yantra is a Sanskrit word meaning 'instrument'. Yantras are diagrams which are believed to possess the power to transform the consciousness of meditators who are sensitive to their potency, having been initiated into knowledge of their symbolism. The design may be drawn, painted, carved, or constructed of sand or earth. The most characteristic design contains either a circle on its own or a circle, interlocking triangles, and a square. The circle represents the universe or the Absolute, the interlaced triangles represent mystical union, and the square represents the earth. The consciousness of the meditator is drawn to the centre of the *yantra*, where often a point (Sanskrit, *bindu*) represents the essence of being. The meditator thus finds his way to the ground of being, the Self that is identical with universal consciousness. The universe itself may be contemplated as a *yantra*, and also the human body, which is viewed as microcosm in macrocosm.

A *mandala* is a type of *yantra. Mandala* is a Sanskrit word meaning 'circle'. The circle is the supreme universal symbol. A circle is self-contained, complete, without beginning and end. In numerous cultures it represents the Absolute, the universe, Heaven, cosmic consciousness, perfection, wholeness, and totality of being.

Mandalas are diagrams and pictures usually contained within a circle. They are often composed of a number of concentric circles and figures, often with a square in the middle representing the earth. They are viewed as three-dimensional by the meditator and he explores them within his consciousness. When the *mandala* is constructed flat on the ground the initiate may penetrate it literally and meditate at its centre. The meditator seeks to become one with the *mandala* and in passing in meditation from the circumference to the centre he experiences the states of being that the internal designs and symbols denote.

The most famous *mandala* is the Buddhist Wheel of Life – the ever-turning wheel of existence. *Mandalas* reach their fullest pictorial and artistic splendour in Tibetan Tantric Buddhism. The baroque designs, flamboyant pictorialism, and brilliant colours of the Tibetan *mandalas* are combined with a rich and powerful symbolism. Moreover, they are superb works of art *per se*. The colours are chosen for their influence on the psyche of the meditator and for their symbolism. Red represents passionate devotion; yellow represents spiritual growth and maturity; gold represents spiritual wealth; sky-blue represents the eternal; and so on.

The lotus flower is a frequent symbol in both Buddhist and Hindu *mandalas*. The lotus is a symbol for enlightenment. The roots of the lotus are in the mud, while its flower opens and displays its beauty above the water. Brahma, the Hindu god of creation, is said to have stood at the centre of a thousand-petalled lotus before bringing the universe into being. And Buddhist legend says of the Buddha that at his birth a large eight-rayed lotus sprang from the earth. The Buddha stepped into the centre and gazed into the ten directions of space – along the eight petals, and upwards and downwards.

In the East it is believed that the *mandala* acts as a bridge between the meditator and the eternal. In a book on the Indo-

Tibetan *mandalas, Theory and Practice of the Mandala* (Rider), Professor Giuseppe Tucci calls them 'psycho-cosmogrammata which may lead the neophyte, by revealing to him the secret play of the forces which operate in the universe and in us, on the way to the reintegration of consciousness'. The theories of the *mandala* originated in India and were taken into Tibet. There are both Hindu and Buddhist *mandalas*, differing at times in style, design, and content, but, as Professor Tucci says: 'As a whole, the spiritual background is the same: the same is the yearning to find out a way from time to eternity, to help the primeval consciousness, which is fundamentally one, to recover its integrity.'

There is, too, a Chinese tradition of the *mandala*. The Chinese mirrors known as TLV mirrors – because their ornamentation looks like the capital letters TLV – are *mandalas*, not sundials as is sometimes suggested. At the centre is the pole star or axis mundi, the Primal Unity or Tao. Outside it is the square representing the earth, and an outer circle represents heaven.

The decoration on a vase or dish can transform these utilitarian objects into *yantras* or *mandalas*. Taoist artists, for example, used marbling on dishes to symbolise *Ch'i* or cosmic energy, turning them into significant forms for visual meditation.

The construction of a *yantra* or a *mandala* is for the artist an act of profound meditation. Similarly, the practice of calligraphy is both an art and a contemplation in Taoism, Zen, and Sufism.

Peter Freuchen, in his *Book of the Eskimos* (Fawcett, New York), describes how the Eskimo meditates before *mandala*-like designs carved on rocks. The creation of the design is itself an act of rapt contemplation that may last several days. The Eskimo sits before a large soft stone and with a small hard stone he slowly carves circles on the stone in front of him while keeping his gaze upon it.

The Shingon Buddhist sect in Japan meditates on *mandalas*. J. Marquès-Rivière, in his *Tantrik Yoga, Hindu and Tibetan* (Rider), says that the Shingon school 'makes use of circles of meditation (*himitsu mandara*), graphic and symbolic, which represent the universe. Mystic letters (the letters of the Sanskrit alphabet) are put in certain places to concentrate the psychic force which issues from the representation. The relationship of these *mandalas* with the Tibetan meditation pictures is re-markable.'

Dr. Carl Jung, the Swiss psychoanalyst, found that *mandalas* appeared in the dreams of some of his patients and some patients also produced them in their paintings. The patients had no prior knowledge of the *mandala*. This led Dr. Jung to see the circle as an archetypal symbol for wholeness of the psyche. It is interesting that Plato said that the psyche was round.

Practice
If possible, place the *yantra* or *mandala* so that its central point (*bindu*) is at eye level, as you sit before it. Its size will determine the number of feet it is away from you – your gaze should be able easily to roam from the centre of the design to its outer edge and

FIG. 6 *Meditation Designs* (From the top: Sufi, Hindu and Christian)

back again to the centre. Sit motionless. The facial muscles should be relaxed, especially those around the eyes. Partly close the eyes if it helps you relax your vision. Rest your gaze on the centre point and then move it outwards slowly to the periphery of the design. As your gaze moves, take in without thought the visual contents of the *yantra* or *mandala*. Then reverse the process and let your gaze travel slowly inwards to the centre. Then close and rest the eyes for a minute or two before repeating the outward and inward journeys of the visual attention. After making this outward and inward movement of the gaze a few times you will find that your attention is attracted to the centre of the design and will effortlessly rest there. Gradually increase the time spent at the centre.

Again the principles of practice described earlier for *trataka* and the *kasina* meditations should be followed. The *yantra* or *mandala* is visualised behind closed eyes and explored with the inner gaze. Eventually the copy-image will be as 'real' as the original and may be reproduced at any time, wherever you may be.

And again sustained contemplation produces a refined image – the 'after-image' or *patibhaga-nimitta* of the Theravada Buddhists This will only come about if the visualisation is effortless and you do not think about the symbols but allow bare attention to move over them. Simply open the mind to the *yantra* or *mandala* and do not anticipate results.

Yantras and *mandalas* often include within their design the letters of the Sanskrit alphabet (even, it seems, in Japan) and meditation centred on them visually is often accompanied by the use of *mantras*. *Yantras* are *looked at*; *mantras* are *listened to*. *Mantras* are sounds, syllables, words, and sentences to be spoken aloud or silently. This is the subject of Chapter 10. A *mantra* may be repeated again and again while a *yantra* or *mandala* is being gazed upon with the eyes open or visualised with the eyes closed. Thus there are four combinations of the dual practice: 1. The *yantra* or *mandala* is gazed upon with the eyes open and the *mantra* is repeated aloud. 2. The *yantra* or *mandala* is gazed upon with the eyes open and the *mantra* is repeated silently. 3. The *yantra* or *mandala* is visualised with the eyes closed and the *mantra* is repeated aloud. 4. The *yantra* or *mandala* is visualised with the eyes closed and the *mantra* is repeated silently. The fourth combination is the most subtle and advanced practice.

Complex Visualisations

In Tantric meditation visualisation is often developed to extra-ordinary degrees of complexity. Complicated *mandalas* are not only visualised in perfect detail with the eyes closed, but are used as a starting point for the unfoldment of their crowded symbolism in what amounts to active psycho-drama.

J. Marquès-Rivière, in *Tantrik Yoga, Hindu and Tibetan* (Rider), says: 'One finds in Tibet the circles of meditation or *kyilkhor*, diagrams, sometimes very large, traced on the earth with powder of different colours, and ornamented with such things as incense sticks and representations of deities (*torma*), made of dough. These diagrams are given by the Master to his disciples as a *ten*, that which concentrates the mind and in which the *manas* (mind) should sink itself, with which it should identify itself.

'Deities – symbolising the forces of the cosmos and of the human being – "come out of" and "re-enter" the *kyilkhor* and the body of the person meditating. There is a constant and living communion between the disciple and his mental creation. Sometimes the whole *kyilkhor* reduces itself to a single point and *enters* into the body of the person meditating and is reabsorbed in him, entering between the two eyebrows.

'The disciple thus learns to "become" the object and to realise the creative power of the mind. Some yogis are even able to create, by the power of the mind, complete beings, living gods, personalities (the *ydam*) which they are afterwards to dissolve. They realise in very truth the illusory nature of all things.'

In some schools of Tantrism practice (Sanskrit, *sadhana*) includes sexual union between men and women as ritual and contemplation. The coupling of gods and goddesses are visualised, their union representing the *unio mystica* that is the goal of all Yogas. When actual coitus between a yogin and a yogini occurs, it is preceded by weeks of meditation and ritual and the union itself is a contemplative act. (See the chapter entitled 'Yoga of Sex: Tantrism' in my *Yoga and Meditation*, Barrie and Jenkins).

Just as in Jnana Yoga the intellect is used to strip the ego of its skins until thought is stilled and the intellect is transcended (see Chapter 8), so the visualisations of Tantric Yoga, however full of intricate imagery they may be in the beginning, usually end with the Void – the formless, imageless experience of pure consciousness. The initial stage of complex visualisation is called 'gross contemplation' (Sanskrit, *sthula dhyana*). The *Gheranda Samhita*, a classic Sanskrit text, provides the following two examples of gross contemplation, from which the advanced powers of visualisation of the Tantric Yogi may be judged:

'*Sthula Dhyana*: Having closed the eyes, let him (the Yogi) contemplate that there is a sea of nectar in the region of his heart: that in the midst of that sea an island of precious stones, the very sand of which is pulverised diamonds and rubies. That on all sides of it, kadamba trees, laden with sweet flowers; that, next to these trees, like a rampart, a row of flowering trees, such as malati, mallika, jati, kesara, campaka, parijata and padma, and that the fragrance of these flowers is spread all round, in every quarter. In the middle of this garden, let the Yogi imagine that there stands a beautiful kalpa tree, having four branches, representing the four *Vedas*, and that it is full of flowers and fruits. Beetles are humming there and cuckoos singing. Beneath that tree let him imagine a rich platform of precious gems, and on that a costly throne inlaid with jewels, and that on that throne sits his particular deity as taught to him by his guru (teacher). Let him contemplate on the appropriate form, ornaments and vehicle of that deity. The constant contemplation of such a form is *sthula dhyana.*

'Another process: Let the Yogi imagine that in the pericarp of the great thousand-petalled lotus (the brain) there is a smaller lotus having twelve petals. Its colour is white, highly luminous, having twelve bija (seed) letters, named ha, sa, ksa, ma, la, va, ra, yum, ha, sa, kha, phrem. In the pericarp of this smaller lotus there are three lines forming a triangle, a, ka, tha; having three angles called ha, la, ksa; and in the middle of this triangle, there is the pranava Om. Then let him contemplate that in that there is a beautiful seat having nada and bindu. On that seat there are two swans, and a pair of wooden sandals. There let him contemplate his guru deva (guardian goddess), having two arms and three eyes, and dressed in pure white, anointed with white sandal-paste, wearing garlands of white flowers; to the left of whom stands Sakti of blood-red colour. By thus contemplating the guru, the *sthula dhyana* is attained.'

The Yogi's guardian (tutelary) god or goddess is a favourite visualisation in Tantric Yoga, and he or she is conjured up before the mind's eye in settings of exotic splendour.

Gross contemplation gives way to two higher stages called the 'luminous' and the 'subtle' – Sanskrit, *jyotir* or *tajo dhyana* and *suksma dhyana*, respectively. An example of the former is to sit motionless with the eyes closed and to contemplate the formless Brahman or Absolute as a clear light. Meditating on Brahman as invisible cosmic energy is subtle contemplation.

The movement of visualisation meditation is from complexity to clearness and voidness, from gross to luminous to subtle. A good example of this is found in *The Tibetan Book of the Dead* (Oxford University Press): 'Whosoever thy tutelary deity may be, meditate upon the form for much time – as being apparent, yet non-existent in reality, like a form produced by a magician . . . Then let the vision of the tutelary deity melt away from the extremities, until nothing at all remaineth visible of it; and put thyself in the state of the Clearness and the Voidness – which thou canst not conceive as something – and abide in that state for a little while. Again meditate upon the tutelary deity; again meditate upon the Clear Light; do this alternately. Afterwards allow thine own intellect to melt away gradually, beginning from the extremities.'

Readers belonging to other cultures may employ the technique described in the preceding paragraph, substituting for the guardian god any image they choose.

Other Forms of Contemplative Visualisation

A Cloak of Light
The average Western meditator should use visualisation tech-

niques that are uncomplicated. In the 'cloak of light' method you sit with the eyes closed and see (with the inner eye) bright pure light covering the entire body and wrapping around the head. G. A. Feuerstein, an authority on techniques of Yoga, says: 'This is perhaps the simplest of all visualisation exercises, and it is conducive to a great inner tranquillity.'

Crystalline Water

In *Yoga* (Teach Yourself) I gave a simple technique of contemplative visualisation of which the aim was to dissolve the phony ego and to reveal the Self. You sit motionless with the eyes closed and then picture every part of your body being filled slowly with water of crystalline clarity, commencing with the head. Next the water slowly fills the space between the throat and the stomach. Then the arms and legs are filled from shoulders to fingertips and from pelvis to toes respectively. The cool pure water also slowly fills the room in which you sit from floor to ceiling.

The second stage of the meditation is to reverse the process witnessed by the inner eye. The water drains slowly from the room, from ceiling to floor. Then the water slowly leaves the legs, the arms, the trunk, and the head. Last of all it disappears from within the skull. At this point, it may be that the false ego slips away also and pure existence remains.

Chakras

An occult form of meditation is visualisation of the *chakras* – 'centres' of psychic energy which some schools of Yoga believe are placed in the astral body between the base of the spine and the crown of the head. In Hindu Tantric Yoga there are seven chief *chakras*. Each has a visual symbol or *yantra* and a sound symbol or *mantra*. The form symbols are circular with from two to sixteen lotus petals on the outside. Each *chakra* has a root letter and its 'vehicle', a dominant colour; its presiding god and goddess or *shakti*; and Sanskrit letters written on the petals. Psychic powers are linked with each *chakra*. (See Chapter 10 of *Yoga* (Teach Yourself, 1979 edition).)

It is customary to start meditating on the lowest *chakra* in the body – the Muladhara, between the anus and the genital organs, visualising its *yantra* and repeating its *mantra* aloud or silently.

Awareness is then taken up the spine, activating each *chakra* in turn. If the meditator is successful in awakening the energy latent in the topmost centre – the Thousand Petalled Lotus Centre (*Sahasrara*), located at the crown of the skull – there is release into spiritual freedom. Sensations of warmth and of light in the area of a 'centre' are reported by meditators, and the body is powerfully energised. Visualisation and repetition of the *mantra* are accompanied by breath controls (*pranayama*) and special postures (*mudras*) and muscular locks (*bandhas*).

The force awakened by meditation on the *chakras* is called Kundalini or Serpent Power by the Hindu Tantric Yogis. It goes by other names in Taoism and Sufism, both of which have similar concepts of energy 'centres' in the body. The guidance of an expert teacher is essential. There have been occasions when individuals have spontaneously exhibited kundalini phenomena.

Visions

The type of visualisation we have described above should not be confused with visions. Involuntary psychic activity, such as visions and locutions, are treated as distractions to meditation in the major religions and therefore they are to be dealt with as a meditator would deal with any other distraction. That is, they are viewed dispassionately and starved of attention and interest – so that, like unwelcome guests, they soon depart.

Finding Suitable Objects for Visual Meditation

It almost goes without saying that the visual forms and symbols chosen by a meditator should be those most significant for *himself*. The *yantras* and *mandalas* of the East have little significance for the average Westerner who has not been initiated into their esoteric meanings. For a Tibetan monk a human skull is a meaningful object for contemplation – but most Occidentals would find this a macabre choice.

For devout Christians the cross is the central *yantra*, but many other designs, works of art, and objects carry for them the force of the holy. It should be noted that the circle on *mandala* motif occurs in the Christian religion – examples being the rose window and the halo. Note, too, that until Carolingian times the equilateral or Greek cross was the Christian symbol, suggesting a *mandala* and centre. Father Herbert Slade, who leads an Anglican order at East Grinstead, Sussex, England, has experimented with combining Christian and Eastern techniques of meditation, including visual meditation. Father Slade's book *Exploring into Contemplative Prayer* (Darton, Longman, and Todd) includes photographs of meaningful visual symbols on which the devout Christian may meditate.

We have seen how Eastern art serves meditation. What of Western art? Abundant symbols may be found in the works of the major and minor artists. You do not need to own an original painting or even a framed reproduction, for photographic book illustration brings the art of mankind – André Malraux's 'museum without walls' – before our eyes. One can look at a picture as a whole or select from within it a significant detail. A patch or a point of colour is enough to provide a colour-*kasina.* Works of art have added significance as objects of meditation if you happen to share André Malraux's belief that 'art is a manifestation of what men are unable to see: the sacred, the supernatural, the unreal – of that which they can see only through art.'

Made One with Nature

Nature supplies the richest fund of objects for visual meditation. The objects of nature are significant for all people, for both the religious and the non-religious. Each object has the resonance of a symbol. Behind each tree or leaf, each rock or pebble, each hill or blade of grass one senses the history of the earth and the mysteries of being and becoming. Contemplation of Nature touches strings deep within the psyche. It is difficult to conceive of any person making the things of Nature the foci of his or her meditation without soon moving towards what Walt Whitman called 'standing at ease in Nature'. And it is a natural step from contemplation of some facet of Nature to being 'made one with Nature' and the mystical.

Rudolf Otto (1869–1937), a German Protestant theologian who made a deep study of both Western and Eastern mysticism, defined nature mysticism as 'the sense of being immersed in the oneness of nature, so that man feels all the individuality, all the peculiarity of natural things in himself'. Professor R. H. Blyth in *Zen in English Literature and Oriental Classics* has written that 'the finest example of nature mysticism' is found in the following lines from William Wordsworth's *The Excursion*:

> *He beheld the sun*
> *Rise up, and bathe the world in light! He looked –*
> *Ocean and earth, the solid frame of earth*
> *And ocean's liquid mass, in gladness lay*
> *Beneath him: – Far and wide the clouds were touched,*
> *And in their silent faces could be read*
> *Unutterable love. Sound needed none*
> *Nor any voice of joy; his spirit drank*
> *The spectacle: sensation, soul and form*
> *All melted in him; they swallowed up*
> *His animal being; in them did he live,*
> *And by them did he live; they were his life . . .*
> *Thought was not; in enjoyment it expired.*
> *No thanks he breathed, he proffered no request;*
> *Rapt in the still communion that transcends*
> *The imperfect offices of prayer and praise.*

Note that '*Thought was not; in enjoyment it expired.*' This is *pure* nature meditation and meditation of the kind that is the main subject of this book. Though in retrospect, as in these famous lines from *Tintern Abbey*, Wordsworth could speak of:

> *A sense sublime*
> *Of something far more deeply interfused,*
> *Whose dwelling is the light of setting suns,*
> *And the round ocean and the living air*
> *And the blue sky, and in the mind of man –*
> *A motion and a spirit, that impels*
> *All thinking things, all objects of all thought,*
> *And rolls through all things.*

Nature mysticism is a form of what is sometimes called 'extrovertive mysticism'. Walter T. Stace explains in *The Teachings of the Mystics* (New American Library): 'The extrovertive way looks outward and through the physical senses into the external world and finds the One there. The introvertive way turns inward, introspectively, and finds the One at the bottom of the self, at the bottom of the human personality . . . The extrovertive mystic with his physical senses continues to perceive the same world of trees and hills and tables and chairs as the rest of us. But he sees these objects transfigured in such manner that the Unity shines through them.'

For Meister Eckhart (circa 1260–1329) 'all blades of grass, wood, and stone, all things are One'. And Jakob Boehme (1575–1624) wrote: 'In this light my spirit saw through all things and into all creatures and I recognised God in grass and plants.' There are, too, the non-theistic nature mystics such as Richard Jefferies and the Zen Buddhists.

There is an understandable tendency for nature mystics to be pantheists – 'the universe is God and God is immanent in all things' – or panentheists – 'God is immanent in all things but also transcendent'. This outlook on Nature and the Universe has inspired some glowing poetry. Listen to this song by Rumi, one of the Sufi poets:

> *I am the dust in the sunlight, I am the ball of the sun.*
> *To the dust I say: Remain. And to the sun: Roll on.*
> *I am the mist of morning. I am the breath of evening.*
> *I am the rustling of the grove, the singing wave of the sea.*
> *I am the mast, the rudder, the steersman and the ship.*
> *I am the coral reef on which it founders.*
> *I am the tree of life and the parrot in its branches.*
> *Silence, thought, tongue, and voice.*
> *I am the breath of the flute, the spirit of man.*
> *I am the spark in the stone, the gleam of gold in the metal,*
> *The candle and the moth fluttering round it,*
> *The rose and the nightingale drunk with its fragrance.*
> *I am the chain of being, the circle of the spheres,*
> *The scale of creation, the rise and the fall.*
> *I am what is and is not. I am – O you who know,*
> *Jaluladdin, O say it – I am the soul in all.*

In the same spirit is the following hymn to 'Brahman Supreme', extracted from the *Svetasvatara Upanishad*:

Thou art the fire,
Thou art the sun,
Thou art the air,
Thou art the moon,
Thou art the starry firmament,
Thou art Brahman Supreme:
Thou art the waters – thou,
The creator of all!
Thou art woman, thou art man,
Thou art the youth, thou art the maiden,
Thou art the old man tottering with his staff;
Thou facest everywhere.
Thou art the dark butterfly,
Thou art the green parrot with red eyes,
Thou art the thunder cloud, the seasons, the seas.
Without beginning art thou,
Beyond time, beyond space.
Thou art he from whom sprang
The three worlds.

(translated by Swami Prabhavananda
and Frederick Manchester)

The objects of nature as the foci for visual meditation are not denied to the modern urban dweller. Facets of nature are found easily by the questing eye: stones, leaves, grass, water, wind, rain, sunlight, and sky. If the worst comes to the worst, a potted plant can represent the countryside, a glass of water the rivers, lakes, and oceans, and anything blue the sky.

'Surprised by Joy'

There is, too, a mysticism of the city, as much poetry and prose testify. In a London tea-shop W. B. Yeats experienced the sudden feeling that he 'was bless¬éd and could bless', and Victor Gollancz tells us, in *My Dear Timothy* (Gollancz), how the sight of an 'ordinary door' at his London club triggered 'joy inexpressible':

'I was in the Royal Automobile Club, of all places, on an afternoon that summer (of 1942), and my eye happened to fall on a door. It was quite an ordinary door, in so far as any single thing in the universe is ordinary, with small panels and big panels and a knob; but I tell you that this door, and the look and the sound and the life of it, filled me with joy inexpressible. And I remember that on the same afternoon, in the same club, I suddenly saw something green through the doors of the winter garden, and saluted it with delighted recognition.'

C. S. Lewis made such moments the most important events in his autobiography, which he called *Surprised by Joy*. It is generally considered that intense moments of joy – 'peak experiences' in the language of the modern psychology of being – are vouchsafed an individual only a few times in a lifetime, if he is lucky. They *happen* – they cannot be summoned up at will. But can, perhaps, such 'peaks' be cultivated? Many of the people who meditate daily report that 'peak experiences' occur more frequently than when they did not meditate. And a few people say they can kindle these experiences by means of techniques of visual meditation.

John Ruskin, the artist and writer, used to heighten perception by throwing his consciousness into objects he observed on his walks. Somewhat similar techniques were practised by John Cowper Powys, the novelist, and by Evelyn Underhill, the writer on Christian mysticism. For the guidance of others, John Cowper Powys and Evelyn Underhill wrote descriptions of the techniques of visual meditation they used. The former called his method 'premeditated ecstasy' and the latter called her meditation 'loving sight'.

Premeditated Ecstasy

John Cowper Powys (1872–1963), whose brothers Theodore Francis and Llewelyn were also prominent men of letters, is best known for such novels as *Wolf Solent, Weymouth Sands,* and *A Glastonbury Romance,* and his *Autobiography*. But he also wrote books expounding a practical philosophy, one of whose names was 'elementalism'. His simple message was that the stresses and strains and frustrations of twentieth-century living – in particular of urban living – could be best countered by contemplation, as opportunity permitted, of the inanimate – of rocks and stones, of earth and water, and of the way sunlight illumines a wall or a door. Contemplation – and living – was something to be enjoyed. That enjoyment was available to all; to the city clerk sitting in a concrete and glass beehive as well as to the farmer and the sailor in more direct touch with the elements. The city dweller can find objects worthy of contemplation in the manner which has already been described above.

Powys's books on 'the art of happiness' were neglected for many years, but they have now been reissued in paperback by the Village Press, London. The style of writing is highly individualistic. In spite of their verbosity, repetitiveness, and now dated 'literary' manner, these philosophical books by John Cowper Powys have a sturdy, earthy wisdom that is winning him new and devoted readers. He recommended a 'psychic-sensuous contemplation' of elemental things. In *A Philosophy of Solitude* (Village Press) he called such contemplation 'premeditated ecstasy'. The technique is a version of the Onion Game that is the subject of Chapter 8. But whereas the Onion Game is most effective looking within to find the no-thingness that is the universal ground of being, John Cowper Powys is concerned with the magic of bare visual attention whereby the most commonplace object can be illumined as though by a light from within and charged with meaningfulness. For example, an 'ordinary door', though now the ecstasy is premeditated and not seemingly fortuitous as it was in the case of Victor Gollancz.

'In all lives,' says John Cowper Powys, 'there is a constant stream of self-consciousness; the person thinking to himself: "Well! here am I, and how difficult my life is!" or on the contrary: "Well! here am I, and how nicely I am getting on!" This feeling of self-awareness is often interrupted by the tension of work, or the tension of society; but even in the midst of work, even in the mids of society, it is constantly coming back, and it always comes back when the work is over and there is a moment of relaxation.

'Even while we are talking to someone, and bestirring ourselves quite actively we feel this self-awareness. And what precisely does it consist of? Glance at the stream of thought passing through at this minute. Much of it – when you have pushed pressing tasks or your immediate struggle aside – is still preoccupation with money-worries and practical worries. But push these aside too? Then begin our poor mortality's emotional pre-occupations. He doesn't love me. She is unfaithful to me. They are solely thinking of themselves in their treatment of me. Oh, how mistaken I was in him! Oh, what a fool I was when I first made love to such a person!

'Well! Get rid of all this from your mind; and with it get rid of all your personal rivalries, ambitions, superiorities, distinctions.

'What is left?

'A few sad, wistful, bitter, desperate, irritable anxieties about people you are fond of.

'Cut that out too. And now what is left?

' "Nothing . . . simply nothing . . . my mind was a perfect blank when you spoke to me."

'But you were staring at the side of the door.

' "Was I? Yes; that is so. I was fascinated by the way that curious light falls just there. I was wondering to myself what made me think of . . . something very long ago."

'Yes; That "Nothing" which you spoke of, as the only thing left, turns out to be that Hegelian "Not-Being" which is the same as "Being". Extract the essence of these two things – your blank mind and the light on the side of the door – and you get that mysterious Becoming, in other words the self encountering the not-self, which if it is not the Absolute is as near to that mystery as we are ever likely to come.'

There is only one thing wrong from our point of view with the above meditation – while practising bare visual attention there should be no 'wondering to myself what it made me think of'. That may come later, after the contemplation of the door has ended. John Cowper Powys frequently intrudes thoughts into what seem otherwise to be accounts of bare awareness. William Wordsworth did the same. These intrusions in both writers are mostly intellectual after-thoughts that get caught up in the texture of the prose or the poetry.

Loving Sight

John Cowper Powys was an independent thinker who believed that life should be enjoyed in spite of the abominable cruelties of the 'First Cause' – he sometimes called his practical philosophy 'in spite of'. In contrast, Evelyn Underhill (1875–1941) was a devout Christian who made a major investigation of the mysticism of the Christian saints. The technique of 'loving sight' which follows is included in her book *Mysticism* (Methuen). Again bare attention is used to intensify the presence and being of objects as we gaze steadily on them. She introduces the subjective emotional factor of 'loving' to add energy and meaningfulness to the meditation – though Eastern masters might say that the love develops of its own accord through sustained contemplative awareness.

'The object of our attention,' she says, 'may be almost anything we please: a picture, a statue, a tree, a distant hillside, a growing plant, running water, little living things.

'Look, then, at this thing which you have chosen. Wilfully yet tranquilly refuse the messages which countless other aspects of the world are sending; and so concentrate your whole attention on this one act of loving sight [so] that all other objects are excluded from the conscious field. Do not think, but as it were pour out your personality towards it: let your soul be in your eyes. Almost at once, this new method of perception will reveal unsuspected qualities in the external world. First, you will perceive about you a strange and deepening quietness; a slowing down of our feverish mental time. Next, you will become aware of a heightened significance, an intensified existence in the thing at which you look. As you, with all your consciousness, lean out towards it, an answering current will meet yours. It seems as though the barrier between its life and your own, between subject and object, had melted away. You are merged with it, in the art of true communion: and you know the secret of its being deeply and unforgettably, yet in a way which you can never hope to express.

'Seen thus, a thistle has celestial qualities: a speckled hen has a touch of the sublime. Our greater comrades, the trees, the clouds, the rivers, initiate us into mighty secrets . . . Life has spoken to life, but not to the surface-intelligence. That surface-intelligence knows only that the message was true and beautiful: no more.'

Every Thing Is A Yantra

Something similar to 'premeditated ecstasy' and 'loving sight' occurs – but *spontaneously*, without summoning the powers of the will – in the masters of mysticism, whose everyday consciousness is infused through and through with pure existence.

C. E. Montague wrote in *A Writer's Notes on his Trade* (Chatto and Windus): 'If form enables matter to rise to the highest achievable power of itself, matter is that in which, alone, form can find exercise for its own transfiguring faculty. In the most perfect picture or book there may be almost no mere matter left; but what has happened is not that matter, in the main, has been expelled; rather, that no considerable margin of matter remains unanimated by form. There is scarcely any mere paint in the Sistine Madonna, but there is plenty of paint.'

We have the evidence of the great masters of meditation that the point can be reached where 'common things' are transformed as 'mere words' are transformed by a Shakespeare or 'mere paint' by a Rembrandt. The analogy with painting is a good one because the great artists transform the most mundane of objects, and not by petty prettifying. Van Gogh's painting of old boots or an 'ordinary' chair are not 'mere paint'. Likewise, when visual meditation is developed to its full depths every thing becomes a *yantra* and there simply are no 'mere things'. It might then be said that every thing the meditator gazes upon turns to gold. At this point we enter what is usually termed the mystical.

Ramana Maharshi said 'every word is a *mantra*'. He might also have said 'every object that can be gazed upon is a *yantra*'. For mystics reach the stage where every object is charged with meaning and every thing is a symbol because it points to a Reality beyond. R. L. Nettleship wrote: 'The True Mysticism is the belief that everything, not being what it is, is symbolic of something more.' There is no need to look for special symbols when you know that all the things you see are profound symbols. No object is unworthy of visual attention. Something of this attitude is found in certain artists. Kandinsky wrote: 'Everything that is *dead* quivers. Not only the things of poetry, stars, moon, wood, flowers, but even a white trouser button glittering out of a puddle in the street.'

There is, too, a more matter of fact reason why *any* object that can be gazed upon for fifteen minutes or more may be effective for visual meditation. Just as any word or sound can act as an effective *mantra*, so any thing that can be gazed upon steadily for the duration of a normal session of meditation elicits the Relaxation Response and the psychological responses that we have called 'mental hygiene'. These psycho-physiological responses operate whatever the intellectual truths or falsities of the claims and interpretations of the mystics.

But the mystics insist, on the basis of their experiences, that there is a mystical dimension in *looking*. They say that to see directly is a special way of *knowing*. Mystical experience is thought by some investigators to be a form of direct perceiving that is not subjected to filtering by the usual mesh of concepts and conditionings. Teresa de Jesus, popularly known as Teresa of Avila, told her disciples: 'I do not require of you to form great and curious considerations in your understanding. I require of you no more than (that) you *look*.'

7

Listening Meditation

1. *Meditate in a place where distractions of noises, voices, and so on are within your tolerance level.*
2. *Sit motionless, poised, and comfortable.*
3. *Breathe quietly, gently, smoothly, and rhythmically. Breathe through the nostrils and down into the abdomen.*
4. *Be quietly aware of any sound that provides a pleasant or neutral auditory stimulus for the duration of meditation.*
5. *Observe a relaxed and passive attitude towards distractions, including thoughts and images that flit in and out of the mind. Each time you become aware that you have 'lost' the sound, return your attention gently to it again. Do this as many times as is necessary, maintaining the relaxed and passive attitude.*

Listening with passive awareness to a constant sound is as effective as looking at an object in producing all the results possible from the practice of meditation. There is some advantage in having the eyes closed throughout the meditation, but suitable sounds for the practice of auditory meditation are not as numerous as objects suitable for visual meditation. Shortly, we shall see some of the way by which Eastern meditators have got round the problem of finding sounds to listen to that are always available.

Suitable Sounds

The ticking of a clock or of a watch or the rhythmical clickety-clack of the wheels of a speeding train heard by its passengers are two examples of the kind of sounds that are suitable for listening meditation. Nature is a rich source of suitable sounds for meditation, provided you are able to meditate within earshot and in comfort and privacy. The advance and retreat of the sea, sucking at pebbles or hissing over sand, provides a satisfying sound for the ear and at the same time a powerful symbol for the person sensitive to Nature's rhythms. The movement of water provides other suitable sounds: purling stream or rushing river, the splashing of a fountain, a waterfall, the patter of rain, and so on. Old Yoga texts advise meditation near waterfalls, rivers, and lakes, as conducive to better health as well as to calming the mind. We know now that the air in such places is high in negative ion concentration, the effect of which is to induce clarity of mind. The chorus of cicadas, the humming of bees, and the chirping of some insects are other sounds of Nature on which the meditative concentration may dwell effortlessly; the songs of birds delight the ear, though one cannot rely on a single feathered songster continuing the song for the full twenty minutes of meditation. Also pleasant for the ear is the soft music the wind makes when using tall grasses or reeds as a harp. Read Zeami's words:

> *Herb or tree,*
> *Earth or sand,*
> *Sough of wind and roar of waters,*
> *Each encloses in itself the Universe;*
> *Spring forests stirring in the eastern wind,*
> *Autumn insects chirping in the dewy grass,*
> *Are they not each a poem?*

On occasions looking and listening meditation may be combined: the glint of sunlight on water and the sound of the moving water, the sight of a bird and its song. As the signs used to say on American railway crossings: *Stop! Look! Listen!*

Here again, in listening meditation, the simple basic rules for practising meditation must be followed – sit still, breathe gently and quietly, attend to the sound with passive awareness, and treat distractions as unimportant.

Listening to Internal Sounds

Hundreds of years ago Indian Hatha Yogis solved the problem

of always having to have a sound to meditate upon available. We saw earlier how our respiratory apparatus provides an ever-ready object for meditative awareness; the Hatha Yogis covered their ears with their hands and listened to sounds within the head and the body that usually go unnoticed.

Employing a profusion of similes, the *Hatha Yoga Pradipika*, a key text of the school of Hatha Yoga, which employs psycho-physiological controls, says that the practice of listening to internal sounds (*nadas*) leads to the experience of *samadhi*, which is blissful absorption in pure consciousness. This is how this text describes this method of meditation: 'The sound which a *muni* (sage) hears by closing his ears with his fingers should be heard attentively, till the mind becomes steady in it. By practising with this *nada* (sound), all other external sounds are stopped . . . In the beginning, the sounds heard are of a great variety and very loud; but as the practice increases they become more and more subtle. In the first stage, the sounds are surging, thundering like the beating of kettle-drums, and jingling ones. In the intermediate stage, they are like those produced by conch, Mridanga, bells, and so on. In the last stage, the sounds resemble those from such things as tinklets, flute, vina and bees. These various kinds of sounds are heard as being produced in the body.'

The technique is to cover the left ear with the left hand and the right ear with the right hand, close the eyes, sit still, breathe smoothly and quietly, and be passively aware of whatever inner sounds may be heard. All external sounds are shut out of the mind. By listening to internal sounds, with the ears covered and the eyes closed, the attention moves effortlessly within.

Readers should close the eyes and the ears only, not the nostrils. In advanced practice, which is worked up to gradually, Hatha Yogis may suspend breathing for several minutes while listening to the *nadas*. This should not be attempted by students who are not being personally instructed by an expert teacher. The meditation can be effective for general use when the breathing is quiet, but not suspended.

In early practice the internal sounds (*nadas*) are coarse and loud, though only in comparison to what they may become with more experience. The old Sanskrit texts compare them to the roaring of an ocean or thunder, kettle drums and trumpets.

With practice, the sounds begin more to resemble flutes and harps and the humming of bees. These descriptions are rather fanciful, but an important principle is demonstrated in the relationship between two contrasting groups of sounds. The principle operates in breathing meditation, visual meditation, devotional prayer, and mantra meditation (including Transcendental Meditation). It is the progressive refinement of whatever stimulus is central in the meditation: a movement from gross to subtle, from breathing to being breathed, from concrete object to an abstraction of the 'after-image', from thought to the source of thought, from the surface mind to pure being.

'Listening in' for the first time to the sounds within the head and body can be a strange experience – but the sounds are never ends in themselves and we should not be seduced by the eloquence of the old Hatha Yoga texts into making them so. That was not the intention of the authors of these texts. Looking for resemblances between the internal sounds and external auditory phenomena during meditation would be to disrupt the meditation – the aim is to listen as far as possible with bare attention, without thinking.

The Unstruck Sound

Subtle sounds are heard within consciousness and are no longer the coarse sounds of bodily processes. Eventually, just as visualised objects refine into subtle abstractions before the mind's eye, so the internal sounds refine until approaching more and more the profoundest sound of all – the 'sound' of silence. Thus the classic Hatha Yoga texts speak of 'the unstruck sound' or 'heart sound' (*anahata nada*). Readers acquainted with the *koan* meditations of Zen may be reminded of the koan 'the sound of one hand (clapping)'.

'The hearing of these (internal sounds) – and similar but different sounds are cited in various accounts – is not an end in itself,' says Ernest Wood in *Yoga* (Penguin Books), 'but only a mode of inward attention to still the outward curiosity of the senses and outward-going tendencies of mental drift. When the practice becomes successful on account of regularity, the last of all the sounds is heard – that from the heart, called the unstruck (*anahata*) sound in contrast to the previous sounds which have died away and been replaced by this.

'The principle is that all attentiveness begins in a starting point, and then proceeds from the coarse to the subtle, and from the subtle to the as yet unknown – the experience *within* the consciousness. The sounds are not in themselves of value. Therefore it is next said that in the sound (*shabda*) of the heart there is a resonance (*dhwani*), in that there is a light (*jyotis*) and in that there is the mind (*manas*). Then, when mind itself disappears (one is no longer thinking of it) there is the veritable supreme place (or rather standing-place) of Vishnu, the very heart and sustaining principle of conscious life.'

According to the Yoga texts, bare awareness of the unstruck or heart sound leads to *samadhi*, a state of pure consciousness in which the duality between subject and object, listener and the sound, is transcended.

'Wherever the mind attaches itself first, it becomes steady there,' says the Hatha Yoga *Pradipika*, 'and then it becomes absorbed in it. Just as a bee, drinking sweet juice, does not care for the smell of the flower; so the mind, absorbed in the *nada*, does not desire the object of enjoyment. The mind, like an elephant, habituated to wander in the garden of enjoyments, is capable of being controlled by the sharp goad of *anahata nada*. The mind, captivated in the snare of *nada*, gives up all its activity; and, like a bird with clipped wings, becomes calm at once. Those desirous of the kingdom of Yoga should take up the practice of hearing the *anahata nada*, with mind collected and free from all cares. *Nada* is the snare for catching the mind; and, when it is caught like a deer, it can be killed also like it. *Nada* is the bolt of the stable door for the horse (the mind of the Yogi). A Yogi should determine to practise constantly in the hearing of the *nada* sounds. The mercury of the mind is deprived of its unsteadiness by being calcined with the sulphur of *nada*, and then it roams supportless in the *akasa* (space) of *Brahman* (the Absolute). The mind is like a serpent; forgetting all its unsteadiness by hearing the *nada*, it does not run away anywhere. The fire, catching firewood, is extinguished along with it (after burning it up); and so the mind also, working with the *nada*, becomes latent along with it. The *antahkarana* (mind), like a deer, becomes absorbed and motionless on hearing the sound of bells, and suchlike; and then it is very easy for an expert archer to kill it.'

Attention to the internal sound having brought peace to the mind, the meditator knows pure consciousness.

Music and Meditation

Professor Wood likens the *anahata* sound to 'the very delicate music of the vina', of which an Indian friend remarked to him: 'While you are listening, you just can't think of anything at all.' 'Those words describe its character very well,' adds Professor Wood. 'Common music stirs or soothes the blood or the nerves, or it tells a story and reminds us of some pleasing and peaceful scene or action, but here there was nothing but music – "music music-born", as Emerson might have put it. Such is the conception of the *anahata* sounds. They are understood to be spiritual sounds, to be tasted as such.'

Western music, too – or at any rate some of it – has the power to induce a thought-free state of pure being. It also, for those persons sensitive to its tones, has the power to communicate states of spiritual consciousness, as J. W. N. Sullivan pointed out in his famous book *Beethoven*: 'We may assume . . . that Beethoven regarded art as a way of communicating knowledge about reality . . . It is true . . . that the artist gives up a superior organisation of experience. But that experience includes perceptions which, although there is no place for them in the scientific scheme, need none the less be perceptions of factors in reality. Therefore a work of art may communicate knowledge. It may indeed be a "revelation". The "higher consciousness" of the great artist is evidenced not only by his capacity for ordering his experience, but also by having his experience. His world may differ from that of the ordinary man as the world of the ordinary man differs from that of a dog, in the extent of his contact with reality as well as in his superior organisation of it.'

How music can communicate states of consciousness, when one considers the manner in which musical sounds are produced (by blowing, striking, scraping), is a great mystery. But one of the reasons that listening to music, in a concert hall or at home playing a record, is so relaxing and refreshing to the spirit is that we usually sit still, breathe quietly, and let the attention dwell effortlessly on the sounds. That is to say, listening to music may be a form of auditory meditation. Boisterous or martial music would not be a suitable choice for meditative listening, but most readers will be familiar with musical works that have the power to soothe and to refresh the spirit.

Mystical Sounds

When Marghanita Laski – *Ecstasy* (Cresset Press) – questioned people about their experiences of ecstasy, she found that music was named as one of the most frequent and powerful triggers of states of joy. Various writers, including mystics familiar with mystical experience, have indicated that music places listeners sensitive to its tones in contact with mystical levels of consciousness.

'All art,' wrote Walter Pater (1839–94) in *The Renaissance*, 'constantly aspires towards the condition of music.' Of all the arts, music most immediately and penetratingly communicates spiritual states. Just as works of art may open the 'inner eye', so may music open the 'inner ear'. Evelyn Underhill wrote: 'Mysticism, the most romantic adventures – from one point of view the art of arts, their source and also their end – finds naturally enough its closest correspondences in the most purely artistic and most deeply significant of all forms of expression. The mystery of music is seldom realised by those who so easily accept its gifts. Yet, of all the arts, music alone shares with great mystical literature the power of waking in us a response to the life-movement of the universe: brings us – we know not how – news of its exultant passions and its incomparable peace. Beethoven heard the very voice of Reality, and little of it escaped when he translated it for our ears.'

Some orders of Sufis use musical sounds to induce states of mystical consciousness: the Sufi dervishes dance to music in a kind of movement meditation. Tibetan Yogis have made a special study of the effects of sound vibrations to alter consciousness.

The music of the Japanese *noh* plays, in which the influence of Zen is apparent, has, according to Zeami (1363–1443) who was a poet and a writer of *noh* plays, the aim of 'opening the ear of the mind'.

Some mystics, and some poets and composers, have claimed the capacity to hear a cosmic quintessential tone. Schumann prefaced his *Fantasia in C Major* with some lines from the poet Schlegel: 'Through all the tones there sounds, throughout the colourful earth, a gentle tone, sustained, for him who listens secretly.' The *anahata* sound is of this nature.

The goal of Chinese philosophical Taoism is a level of being in tune with the Tao, the universal Way of Nature. The Taoist philosopher Chuang Tzu illustrated this goal with the following story:

'A disciple said to Lu Chu: "Master, I have attained to your Tao. I can do without fire in winter. I can make ice in summer."

' "You merely avail yourself of latent heat and latent cold," replied Lu Chu. "That is not what I call Tao. I will demonstrate to you what my Tao is."

'Thereupon he tuned two lutes, and placed one in the hall and the other in the adjoining room. And when he struck the *kung* note on one, the *kung* note on the other sounded; when he struck the *chio* note on one, the *chio* note on the other sounded. This because they were both tuned to the same pitch.

'But if he changed the interval of one string, so that it no longer kept its place in the octave, and then struck it, the result was that all the twenty-five strings jangled together. There was sound as before, but the influence of the key-note was gone.' (Chuang Tzu xxiv. Trans. H. A. Giles.)

The Power of Silence

In music that has the power to move us deeply, the silences between the notes and passages seem to have more influence than the notes themselves. The mystic masters say that it is not in sounds, but in silence, which is paradoxically a kind of music, that God or the Absolute or pure Being may be found.

The highest forms of listening meditation is awareness of silence – 'silence listening to silence'.

8

Who (or What) am I?
The Onion Game

BASIC TECHNIQUE

1. *Meditate in a place where distractions of noise, voices, and so on are within your tolerance level.*
2. *Sit motionless, poised, and comfortable.*
3. *Breathe quietly, gently, smoothly, and rhythmically. Breathe through the nostrils and down into the abdomen.*
4. *Turn your attention inwards and seek deep within yourself the answer to the question 'Who (or What) am I?'. Strip the ego-onion of its skins by discarding as 'not-I' things the body, the senses, the mind, and all the conditionings that make up the concept of an ego. Finally you hold in your mind the naked question 'Who?' or 'What?'. Dwell in the pure being that results when all the ego's skins have been discarded, including the question itself.*
5. *Distractions and wandering away from the pursuit of your true Self beyond the ego should be treated in the relaxed way that has been described for all the other methods of meditation. A calm and passive attitude is maintained throughout the meditation.*

The Deepest of Mysteries

Arthur Schopenhauer (1788–1860), the German philosopher, was attracted to Eastern mysticism. He used to pass into deep meditation when taking walks. Once, in a park, he wandered into the centre of a flower-bed and stood there in rapt concentration. An angry park-keeper shouted: 'Who do you think you are?' Schopenhauer replied: 'Ah! If only I knew.' And Thomas Carlyle (1795–1881), at the age of eighty, as he towelled following a bath, is said to have plucked his dried-up skin and roared: 'What the devil then am I?'

Here is the profoundest of mysteries. Sartre and some other Western existentialist philosophers have explored the nature of consciousness and found an emptiness, a kind of hole at the centre of being. Their reaction has not been the robust anger of Carlyle but anxiety, despair, and a sense of absurdity. In contrast, Hindu, Buddhist, and Taoist Yogis, and Sufic and Christian mystics, have made the same inner journey into the Void and experienced bliss consciousness, fullness, the heaven that lies within and the peace that passeth understanding. They are in accord with the *Tao Te Ching* (c. 240 BC) when it says: 'Where the mystery is the deepest is the gate to all that is subtle and wonderful.'

This meditation differs from the others in this book in that some meditation in the dictionary sense of 'thinking about' is called for. Here, however, a thorn is being used to extract a thorn from the skin. For the intellect is used to eliminate, to cut away and to clear spaces, so that finally thought transcends itself and the ground of being is known. The process of cutting away may be likened to peeling an onion until the last skin is discarded – hence the technique may be dubbed 'the Onion Game'.

The Onion Game

The Onion Game is a form of the Master Game – see *The Master Game* (Dell, New York) – that Robert S. de Ropp has written about. Its aim is 'awakening' or 'enlightenment'. He places it above the Religion Game, whose aim is salvation. It is played alone, sitting still with the back upright, in a place as quiet and restful as possible. It is a solitary quest that takes awareness beyond the clamour, clutter, and confusion of the ego into the clear space and white light of pure consciousness. It is as though the meditator has stepped into a clearing in a dense jungle and is able to look up at the sky. To dissolve the ego is not annihilation or surrender to nihilism, masters of the meditation tell us, but the discovery of the Self beyond the ego. The starting point is the question: 'Who (or What) am I?'

Mystics of all cultures have been centrally concerned with the problem of identity, with the nature of man's innermost being. The *Who (or What) am I?* meditation is found in the spiritual practices of Hinduism, Buddhism, and the other major Eastern religions. Like their Hindu and Buddhist counterparts, the mystics of Islam have sought to answer this question and have followed the meditative technique for uncovering one's real nature that we have called the Onion Game. The culmination of this meditation is discovery of that which we really are, and which at the same time is that which we have always been. The illusion that the Self is the ego is the ignorance – or ignore-ance – that has to be removed. A concise and crisp Sufic text gives a perfect summary of the method:

> *I am not the body*
> *I am not the senses*
> *I am not the mind*
> *I am not this*
> *I am not that.*
> *What then am I? What is the self?*
> *It is in the body*
> *It is in everybody*
> *It is everywhere*
> *It is the All.*
> *It is Self. I am It. Absolute Oneness.*

> > (Quoted F. C. Happold,
> > *Prayer and Meditation*,
> > Penguin Books.)

In this meditation you sit in a quiet place and question yourself. The 'I' proves impossible to find, but we can perceive all the things with which it is falsely identified. Each question and answer strips the ego-self of a skin. Finally, when the last skin has been discarded we find the Self beyond the ego – '*I am*'*-ness* or pure existence – which has been there all the time. Strip an onion entirely of its skins and *nothing* remains. What remains when the ego, the illusory 'I', is stripped of its skins is also nothing – or rather *no thing* – which mystics yet say is everything. Absolute Oneness.

I am not the body

Parts of the body may be amputated – an arm, a leg, or both arms and both legs. The cells of the body are in continual process of repair and renewal. But the 'I' is not diminished in the least by the loss of limbs or by the changes in the cells of the body. Even damage to part of the brain may leave the 'I' untouched. Looking over a photograph album, we perceive how body and face have changed with the years. Yet through all the changes, and through all the minutes, hours, days, weeks, months, and years of living, the sense of 'I' persists unchanged.

I am not the senses

The senses, too, may be lost without diminishing the 'I'. Becoming blind or deaf does not close down or shut out any part of our feeling of 'I-ness' – as can be tested instantly by covering the eyes or the ears.

I am not the mind

What of the mind? Is not the mind the 'I'? 'I think, therefore I am,' said Descartes. But here, too, when we observe the mind we perceive change. The 'I' is not the procession of images that come and go on the screen of the mind, though the authentic Self is the light by which the images are projected. The 'I' is not the emotions which pass like wind-driven clouds across the clear sky of pure consciousness. Our feelings are in a constant state of flux. Moods come and go, often without warning and often without any justification that the conscious mind can discern. Our feelings about things alter with age and sometimes dramatically by the hour. There is nothing solid here on which to base a self. Nor should we identify with our thoughts which, like other contents of the mind, can be passively observed.

An Eastern technique for finding pure awareness is to sit still and calmly and passively observe the activity within the mind. There should be no interference with the flow of thought and no judgements passed on what is observed. Note how thoughts arise and how they give rise to associated thoughts. Watch the thoughts cross the mind and vanish as dispassionately as you would watch flying geese cross the sky. Passive awareness is the key to success in this meditation. Progress is made when thoughts, starved of the customary interest and reaction, quieten and become fewer. Gaps of pure awareness open up between thoughts. Eventually pure consciousness may last for several seconds and later for several minutes, the mind silent yet awake and alert.

The above method of meditation has two principal aims. The first is to quieten the mind. The second is to make the meditator aware of the Silent Witness or Unseen Observer, which is also called the Self.

The 'I' cannot be the contents of the mind, for they can become objects of awareness. That which, in essence, each of us *is* can only be known when thought falls silent and the mind has been emptied of its contents. The Self is not the ego, but what remains when the ego has been stripped of all its skins? When the last skin of an onion has been thrown away, nothing remains. So, too, when the ego is stripped of all its conditioned skins, nothing remains – or rather *no thing*. The Self is no thing. A thing is *phenomenon*, whereas the Self is *noumenon*.

I am not this, I am not that

The authentic 'I' should not be identified with all those attitudes and beliefs that are among the skins of the ego. Nor with the social roles we act out on the stage of life. Nor with our memories. Nor with concepts based on our layers of knowledge.

The ego arises through false identification with the body, emotions, thoughts, actions, goals, loves, hates, hopes, fears, pleasures, pains, memories, ideas, and special roles – through false identification with all our conditions. Reflection shows that each of these cannot be the Self. No more can their sum total be the authentic Self. The Self, our true nature, is beyond the ego.

What then am I? What is the Self?

The Self cannot be an object of the ego and so cannot be described the way *things* are described. The Self, as we said, is no thing. The Self transcends the subject-object duality and cannot be known by the mind. But through techniques of meditation the obstacles to awareness of the Self are dissolved and 'the Self knows the Self'.

It is the All. Absolute Oneness

As the mystic holds that each person's essential and authentic nature is that of the universe, the enquiry 'Who (or What) am I?' is part of the *via negativa*, the mystical way to the Absolute or God through negation, through saying 'not this, not that'.

The 'no thing' that remains when the 'not-I' process has been taken to its conclusion is the Self or *Atman* which Hindu Vedanta says is *Brahman*, the universal spirit or consciousness. It is also the 'Buddha nature', Meister Eckhart's Godhead, and so on. The Onion Game is yet another form of emptying the mind and experiencing what some mystics have called 'the union of nothing with nothing'. It differs from most other methods of mystical meditation in making use of the sharp knife of the intellect to cut a way to the centre of the mystery of being.

Master Players

An essential way to mastering any sport or craft or art is to observe the masters in action and to copy their movements. This is true also of the Onion Game. In this chapter we shall observe how a few masters pursue the 'Who (or What) am I?' enquiry. The reactions of readers is sure to vary in the extent to which this line of appeal is meaningful and effective. Not everyone is comfortable with the intricacies of this intellectual approach, nor are intellectuals always happy with the logic of the argument, or at any rate with that of *every* celebrated player. For them there are the awareness techniques described elsewhere in this book. But some readers will find the Onion Game, as played by its masters, penetratingly meaningful.

Knowing the Self

If we are to consult the most skilful exponents of the Onion Game, we must begin with the forest sages who wrote the Hindu *Upanishads*. The first *Upanishads* are thought to have been written about 800 BC. They are mainly taken up with instruction in finding the *Atman* or Self beyond the ego and with the doctrine that Self (*Atman*) equals Overself (*Brahman*). *Brahman* is universal spirit or consciousness and alone is the ultimate reality.

The *Upanishads* provide the oldest surviving accounts of the 'not this, not that' technique for cleansing the ego and knowing the Self or pure consciousness. In the *Upanishads* the 'inmost centre', the abode of the Self, is described as 'the space within the heart'. The *Chandogya Upanishad*, believed to be one of the earliest *Upanishads*, provides in its eight sections a classic account of how to uncover the *Atman*. The sage Prajapati is instructing Indra, his main pupil. He tells him to eliminate false identification with the body, with the senses, and with thought, so as to enter the state of spiritual freedom that is the goal of all the Yogas.

JNANA YOGA

Finding one's true nature is the goal of all the Yogas. Reaching the goal through the knowledge and insight triggered by the meditation we have called the Onion Game is for the Hindu a form of Jnana Yoga, the Yoga of knowledge of the Self. It does not exclude the methods of other Yogas – such as the devotional worship of Bhakti Yoga, the selfless activity of Karma Yoga, or the body mastery of Hatha Yoga – but the distinctive character of Jnana Yoga stems from the use of study and reflection to sweep away all mental obstacles to the realisation of pure existence. The Jnana Yogi is taught to cut a way through the mental impressions or *samskaras* which prevent him seeing the light of pure conscious ness. The intellect is welcomed as a tool which 'opens out a way' to that 'inmost centre' which Robert Browning wrote of in his poem *Paracelsus*:

> *Truth is within ourselves; it takes no rise*
> *From outward things, whate'er you may believe.*
> *There is an inmost centre in us all,*
> *Where truth abides in fullness; and around,*
> *Wall upon wall, the gross flesh hems it in,*
> *This perfect, clear perception – which is truth.*
> *A baffling and perverting carnal mesh*
> *Binds it, and makes all error: and, to* KNOW

Rather consists in opening out a way
Whence the imprisoned splendour may escape,
Than in effecting entry for a light
Supposed to be without.

The meditation that is the subject of this chapter sets out to demolish the walls brick by brick.

A section of the *Bhagavad Gita*, a work much loved by the Hindus, is given to Jnana Yoga. It makes clear that intellect (*buddhi*) should be esteemed, being superior to mind (*manas*), just as mind is superior to the senses, which are themselves superior to the physical body. But superior even to intellect is transcendental consciousness, which is knowing the Self. Classical Yoga refers to this level of awareness as bliss consciousness (*sat chit ananda*).

If the Self is not the body and not the ego, then the Self is detached from the actions of the body and those volitional actions that appear to be directed by the ego. In the section on Jnana Yoga in the *Gita*, Lord Krishna instructs Arjuna: 'He who can see inaction in action, who can also see action in inaction, he is wise among men, he is devout, he is the performer of all action.' (Discourse iv, 18).

Shankara (c.799–820AD), the Hindu philosopher who is probably the greatest teacher of Jnana Yoga, wrote a commentary on the *Gita*, and had this to say about the verse quoted above:

'Now, action which belongs to the body and the senses, while yet retaining its own nature as action, is falsely imputed by all to the Self who is actionless and immutable; whence even a learned man thinks "I act". Hence the passage means: He who sees inaction in action, i.e., he who has the right knowledge that action, which is commonly supposed by all to pertain to the Self, does not really belong to the Self, just as motion does not really pertain to the trees (on the shore of the river) which appear (to a man on board the ship) to move in the opposite direction; and he who sees action in inaction, i.e., he who knows that even inaction is action – for inaction is but a cessation of bodily and mental activities, and like *action* it is falsely attributed to the Self and causes the feeling of egoism as expressed in the words "quiet and doing nothing, I sit happy" – he who can realise the nature of action and inaction as now explained is wise among men; he is devout (Yogi), he is the performer of all actions. He is released from evil; he has achieved all.' (A. M. Sastri, Jr., *The Bhagavad Gita*, Mysore.)

The actionless and immutable nature of the Self and the Self's inaccessibility to the senses is brought out earlier in the *Bhagavad Gita* (in Discourse ii, 20–25). It should be remembered that the following discourses take place shortly before a battle.

20. He is not born, nor does He ever die; after having been, He again ceases not to be; nor the reverse. Unborn, eternal, unchangeable and primeval, He is not slain when the body is slain.

21. Whoso knows Him as indestructible, eternal, unborn and inexhaustible – How, O son of Pritha, and whom, does such a man cause to slay, and whom does he slay?

22. Just as a man casts off worn-out clothes and puts on others which are new, so the embodied Self casts off worn-out bodies and enters others which are new.

23. Him, weapons cut not; Him, fire burns not, and Him, water wets not; Him, wind dries not.

24. He cannot be cut, nor burnt, nor wetted, nor dried up. He is everlasting, all-pervading, stable, firm, and eternal.

25. He, it is said, is unmanifest, unthinkable and unchangeable . . .

Shankara comments on ii, 24: 'As the Self is inaccessible to any of the senses, He is not manifest. Wherefore, He is unthinkable. For that alone which is perceived by the senses becomes an object of thought. Verily, the Self is unthinkable, because He is inaccessible to the senses. He is unchangeable. The Self is quite unlike milk, which, mixed with buttermilk, can be made to change its form. He is changeless also because He has no parts; for, whatever has no parts is never found to undergo change. Because the Self is changeless, He is unchangeable.'

The transcendental nature of the Self and its oneness with *Brahman* is central to Yoga and indeed provides its *raison d'être*.

Ramana Maharshi

In recent times the leading Hindu exponent of the Onion Game has been Ramana Maharshi (1879–1950). Like Shankara, Ramana Maharshi was a Jnana Yogin and his philosophy that of Advaita Vedanta – basically non-duality and the equation Self equals Brahman. To all his questioners he advised the practice of 'Who am I' meditation. This enquiry was the essence of his teaching. Its aim – to realise the Self to be found in pure consciousness.

Ramana Maharshi told his pupils to say: 'The body and its functions are not "I".' Likewise: 'The feelings are not I.' And: 'The thoughts are not I.' He also told his pupils to trace the feeling of 'I' to its substratum, the ground of being; 'The Self is the pure Reality in whose light the body, the ego and all else shines.' He taught that 'When thoughts are stilled, pure consciousness remains over', and that 'Reality is only one and that is the Self. All the rest are mere phenomena in it, of it, and by it. The seer, the objects, and the sight, all are the Self only.' This is the non-duality of Advaita Vedanta.

Ramana Maharshi also taught that thoughts originate in the ground of one's being and should in meditation be traced to their source. He told pupils to observe how a thought arises and to ask: 'To whom has this thought occurred?' 'To me.' But 'Who am I?' Today Maharishi Mahesh Yogi has the same message – follow thought to its source in pure being. But his method of meditation is different. (See Chapter 10.)

Quest For The Overself

The books of Dr. Paul Brunton have enjoyed great success and been in print for many years. In writing about Yogic meditation based on Vedanta, he avoids Sanskrit words and abstruse terminology. The technique of meditative self-analysis that is likened to skinning an onion features prominently in his books *The Secret Path* and *The Quest for the Overself*, concisely in the former and in detail in the latter. The Self beyond the ego, the

Hindu Atman, he calls the Overself, indicating its transcendental and cosmic dimension. The progressive stages of cleansing the ego into no-thingness, as described by this popular writer, follow the classic descriptions in the *Upanishads* and match the Sufic summary of the method quoted near the start of this chapter. That is to say, the 'I' is successively noted as not the body, not the feelings, and not the intellect. Dr. Brunton – wisely in my opinion – recommends supporting self-analysis with regulating and following the breath. Introspective analysis is rarely enough in itself to dissolve the hard shell of the ego. The techniques of meditation described elsewhere in this book combine well with intellectual enquiry into the underlying basis of being which mystics call the Self, the Witness, the Spectator, and so on. The intellect, having been taken to its limits of penetrating usefulness, surrenders to pure awareness and the mind is calmed for intuitive enlightenment.

I Am Not The Body

'We cannot be body alone because,' says Dr. Brunton in *The Secret Path*, 'when a man's body is completely stricken with paralysis, even his sight, touch, hearing, taste and smell destroyed, he yet remains undiminished as a self-conscious being. Strike off both his hands, both his legs, take his eyes and parts of his other organs – still he does not feel less than himself, still the sense of "I" is as strong as ever.'

Is the 'I' the brain? Large tracts of memory may become inaccessible to consciousness, but the sense of 'I' continues.

'The conclusion is that since both the separate parts and separate senses of the body are not the self, then their totality – the entire body itself, the aggregate of senses and limbs and organs – cannot possibly be the conscious real self,' says Dr. Brunton in *The Quest for the Overself*. And he goes on: 'The self is *not* the body, but a conscious entity, that which becomes one with the body when fully plunged into it.'

I Am Not The Feelings

The emotions, too, are 'not-I' phenomena. There are times when we observe our emotions as though they are no more to us than the clothes we are wearing. Moods and emotions come and go like colours on a screen before the eyes, but the sense of 'I' remains unchanged. 'The fact of my awareness of emotions does not mean that they constitute my self. The existence of someone who feels is one thing whilst his self-awareness is quite another.' (Dr. P. Brunton in *The Quest for the Overself*.)

I Am Not The Mind

The third stage in this meditation is to ask: 'Am I the thinking intellect?' 'Watch your intellect in its working,' says Dr. Brunton, in *The Secret Path*. 'Note how thoughts follow one another in endless sequence. Then try to realise that there is someone who thinks. Now ask: "Who is this Thinker?" Who is this "I" that sleeps and wakes up; that thinks and feels; that works and speaks? What is it in us that we call the "I"? . . . If you will but steadfastly regard the mystery that is in you, the divine mystery in man, it will eventually yield and display its secret.'

Mystics of many lands, throughout recorded history, have said that thought can be silenced and that with thinking in abeyance a person's true nature is revealed. Silencing thought is not unconsciousness but pure consciousness, a bright crystalline awareness.

What Then Am I? What Is The Self?

'The world is in a continual condition of flux, and man himself seems to be a mass of changing emotions and thoughts. But if he will take the trouble to make a deep analysis of himself, and to ponder that there is a part of himself which receives the flow of impressions from the external world, and which receives the feelings and thoughts that arise therefrom. This deeper part is the true being of man, the unseen witness, the silent spectator, the Overself.' (Dr. P. Brunton in *The Secret Path*.)

Tennyson wrote:

If thou would'st hear the Nameless, and wilt dive
Into the Temple-cave of thine own self,
There, brooding by the central altar, thou
May'st haply learn the Nameless hath a voice,
By which thou wilt abide, if thou be wise.

Straining to look at the Self is like trying to see one's own face without a mirror or any reflecting surface. But Yoga and the other mystical systems say that the Self (or Overself) can be known by a process of elimination, of stripping away all that it is not, 'not this, not that', and by meditative awareness. Attention is the key to knowing the Self intuitively. 'Attention is the soul adhering in matter,' says Dr. Brunton in *The Quest for the Overself*, '*and therefore one plane higher than thought*.' Through the application of Right Attention 'the hidden self discloses itself spontaneously. And we need not imagine this self to be some figment of the metaphysical imagination. On the contrary, because it is the innermost centre which vibrates behind and through thinking, feeling and acting, it must be the highest intensity of our individual life.'

Gentle Breathing

Dr. Brunton advises that the 'Who am I?' enquiry, as outlined above, should be followed immediately by awareness of quiet slow breathing. You breathe through both nostrils, exhaling and inhaling gently and holding the breath momentarily in between. The flow of breath is given full attention while you sit comfortably with the eyes closed. 'It is important that the student should pour all his consciousness into his breathing until he seems to live in it for the time being . . . He may take it as a sign of success when the breath rhythm flows gently and effortlessly so that if a feather were held before the nostrils it would not move.' The student should continue meditative concentration 'so that he feels that he has become a "breath-being", as it were. He steeps himself utterly in the changed breathing process, blends his mind with it, submerges all other thoughts into watching it, and so becomes temporarily transformed into a subtler, more sensitive person. Such a stage is not reached immediately, but follows after weeks of regular practice.

'The power of this single exercise over the mind can scarcely be appreciated by those who have not practised it. It restores a harmonious rhythm to the human machine. It can transform an agonised heart into a heart at peace with the world.' (Dr. P. Brunton in *The Secret Path.*)

Awakening To Intuition

Having calmed the nervous system and mind with awareness of
breathing for at first five and later fifteen or twenty minutes, the
third and final step in Dr. Brunton's method is 'the awakening
to intuition'. He tells us to make a humble request, a half-prayer
to the Overself in the centre of our being 'to reveal its existence'.
'Wait expectantly, even confidently.' 'Listen-in' for a response.
Wait two or three minutes. Repeat the question and wait again
for three or four minutes. Finally, question and wait again, with
poised and open awareness, for about five minutes. 'The response
of awakening intuition may come the first time this exercise
is practised, or it may not come until after several weeks or
even months of daily practice.' (Dr. P. Brunton in *The Secret
Path.*)

The Illusory Ego

'I can never catch my *self*,' said the philosopher David Hume
(1711–76). 'Whenever I try, I always stumble at some sense-
impression or idea.' And William James observed: 'The so-called
"self" is only a stream of thought; the passing thought itself is
the thinker.' Other Western philosophers have been perplexed
and disquieted by their inability to grasp the 'I.' Eastern philosophers, who have looked within themselves since antiquity,
have not felt any unease at the insubstantiality of what they have
seen. Indeed, they have responded with feelings of tranquillity
rather than of angst. For they have held that the ego is illusory
and has no real existence except as a concept. There is no ego-
self. There is only Brahman, Tao, the Void – formless, changeless, and eternal. 'Under whatever name and form one may
worship the Absolute Reality,' said Ramana Maharshi, 'it is
only a means for realising It without name and form. That alone
is true Realisation, wherein one knows oneself in relation to that
Reality, attains peace and realises one's identity with It.'

It is very difficult for the average Westerner to begin contemplating the possibility that he has no 'I' or 'me' in the sense
of an ego-self. If a person is in bondage to the idea that he has
an ego which directs his actions, then the Buddhist doctrine of
non-ego (Pali, *anatta*) is baffling. Christmas Humphreys in

Buddhism (Penguin Books), explains this key Buddhist doctrine as follows: 'Examine the five ingredients of the man we know, said the Buddha, and you will find a body (*rupa*); sensation, in the sense of emotional reaction (*vedana*); the mind's reaction to sense stimuli (*sanna*); the mental processes based on pre-dispositions (*sankharas*); and consciousness (*vinnana*). All these without exception are in a state of flux, and even the body, the grossest of them, is utterly changed each seven years. Where, then, is the "immortal soul"? If the personality be called the self, it is perishing hour by hour; if the character, the individuality, be called the self, the same applies, though far more slowly. What, then, of a SELF? If by this be meant the principle of Enlightenment, or Life itself, it is not the property of man or of any man. To the extent that it is part of man, one of his faculties, it is not immortal; to the extent that it is immortal it is not the property of any man. Yet if there be nothing which, within the illusion of manifestation, grows and moves towards Enlightenment, what of the Noble Eightfold Path to the Goal? Who treads it – what walks on? The answer is consciousness, the integrating factor or Self which, subject like all else to *anicca*, change, and *dukkha*, suffering, is unquestionably *anatta*, lacking a permanent immortal something which separates it from the Whole.'

Wei Wu Wei

T. J. Gray, writing under the pseudonym Wei Wu Wei, takes an intellectual rapier to the ego-onion and flenses it with short swift strokes. (*Wue-wei* is the Chinese doctrine of 'non-action'). In the preface to *The Tenth Man* (Hong Kong University Press), he wrote: I have only one object in writing books: to demonstrate that there could not be anyone to do it.' The 'me' that we think we are is only a concept, he says. 'Totality of understanding' brings freedom from bondage to the ego. People can be liberated by 'comprehending their own total inexistence as autonomous entities, which comparison, by abruptly snapping the phenomenally interminable chain of conceptualisation, would reveal the noumenality whose immensity is all that they are.' The personality is just a concept. 'This exercise of supposed choice and decision, this series of perpetual acts of will or of wilfulness, called "volition", is what constitutes bondage, and the ensuing conflict, experienced as suffering, is due to the supposed *need* to act volitionally. And the abandonment of this nonsense must abolish the cause of bondage, bondage being bondage to volition experienced as "I", and implying the phenomenal object concerned. With the understanding of the incongruity of this notion nothing is left to be bound, and nothing is left that can suffer as "me" . . . What I am is expressed phenomenally as see-ing, hear-ing, feel-ing, taste-ing, smell-ing, think-ing, but there is no objective "I" that sees, hears, feels, tastes, smells or thinks . . . Objects "live" sensorially or are "lived" sensorially, and what I am is their sentience.'

Two characteristic examples of Mr Gray's aphoristic style will show why he delights some readers and is incomprehensible to others:

WHO?

I cannot *say* it,
I cannot *know* it,
I cannot *be* it,

Because I *am* it,
And all it is I am.

(*The Tenth Man,* Hong Kong University Press.).

I—I THIS UNIVERSE WHICH WE ARE

When SUBJECT looks – subject sees object.
When subject is seen looking at object
Subject becomes object, and is no longer subject.

When subject looks at itself, it no longer sees anything,
for there cannot be anything to see, since subject, not
being an object as subject, cannot be seen.
    That is the 'mirror-void' – in the absence of anything seen,
of anything seeable, which subject is.
    But it is neither 'mirror' nor 'void' nor any thing at all.
It is not even 'it'.
    That is the transcendence of subject and object – which is
pure is-ness.

That is what is – the total absence which is the presence
of all that seems to be.

Perhaps it could be said better, but there can be little
more to be said.

(*Open Secret*, Hong Kong University Press.)

Note that in the title of the second extract Mr. Gray uses 'I–I',
which was Ramana Maharshi's term for the ultimate Self. He
adds a footnote, remarking that 'The "mirror-void" is a re-
splendant shining mirror which reflects the phenomenal universe,
revealing every thing and retaining no thing.'

'One Hand Clapping'

Wu Wei Wu writes in the spirit of Zen (Chinese, *Ch'an*). The
goal of Zen meditation is to see into your 'True-nature' or
'Buddha-nature'. This is seen in the *koans* or meditation problems given by Zen masters to their pupils. The *koans* are a kind
of riddle on which discursive thought cannot obtain a grasp.
Man's essential nature is beyond thought and is an experience
of his identity with the universe. The primary *koan* is 'MU'
which means 'nothing' or 'no thing'. Others are 'What is my
original face before I was born?', 'From where you are, stop
the distant boat moving across the water', 'Who is it that hears?',
and 'What is the sound of one hand clapping?'

The *koan* is not thought about. It is held 'in the belly', and
the meditator awaits the awakening to enlightenment (*satori* or
kensho). Finding universal identity is usually joyous and marked
by heightened perception of the external world. It is a totally
new viewpoint. The *satori* experience is deepened by further
meditation and insights. Sometimes enlightenment occurs during
meditation and sometimes it is triggered by a commonplace sight
or sound.

The pupil has regular private interviews with the Zen master
or *roshi*, who demands a spontaneous answer to the *koan*. As the
nature of the *koan* precludes intellectual solution, the authentic
answer is often a gesture or action. The Zen master is said to be
able to discern whether or not a pupil is enlightened from the
way he walks into the teaching chamber.

In *The Three Pillars of Zen* (Beacon Press, Boston), Philip Kapleau gives transcripts of interviews between the Zen master Yasutani-roshi with Western pupils. One pupil who was not making progress with the primary *koan* 'MU' was told to use 'Who am I?' as her *koan*, later shortening it to 'Who?'. The Zen master said that asking 'Who am I?' 'is really no different from asking 'What is MU?'

In one form of mobile Zen the *koan* is carried into everyday activity. The questions are asked: 'Who is walking?', 'Who is eating?', 'Who is shaving?', 'Who is doing the housework?', 'Who is watching television?', 'Who is going to sleep?', and so on.

Alan Watts

Alan Watts, who was for some years an Episcopalian minister, wrote a series of zestful books interpreting Zen, Vedanta, and Taoism for Western readers. Like Wei Wu Wei, he aims to bring about 'totality of understanding' in his reader, through jolting him out of the illusion that he is divorced from everything in the universe and exists as a separate 'skin-encapsulated ego'. He, too, taught that there is no 'I' that feels or thinks, but only feel-ing and think-ing.

In the following passage from *The Supreme Identity* (Wildwood House), Alan Watts highlights the difference between the ego and the Self:

'By simple introspection we may come to a preliminary understanding of what is meant by the Self as distinct from the ego or particular individuality. This understanding will, however, be in the nature of a "non-idea", because we shall have to think of the Self in terms of what it is not. We begin with the principle that there is a distinction (not of opposition, but of transcendence) between subject and object, knower and known. A light illumines things other than itself, and the eye sees things other than itself; what is seen, then, is not the seer.

'Man is aware of his own body, potentially if not actually. By sight and touch he can know its whole exterior surface, and by internal sensations, by pains in the head and other organs, by moods and emotions, by dreams and other psycho-physical phenomena, he becomes aware of its interior functioning. An emotion, for example, is a true "feeling" of the inside of the brain; one does not have to get at it with the fingers! If he has physiological knowledge he can concentrate attention or interior feeling on almost any organ in the physical system. [Such awareness is cultivated to an extreme degree in the practice of *hatha-yoga* . . . The object of *hatha-yoga*, aside from mere physical culture, is to acquire a very thorough knowledge of the distinction of the Self from the internal organs.] In the same way he is, or can be, aware of the psychological patterns of thought and feeling which constitute his individual character – his ideas, emotions, and desires – constituting the soul. In sensing, feeling, thinking, he knows, not "I am sensing, feeling, thinking," but "I am aware of the senses, the feelings, and the mind interacting with their objects".

'Now what John Smith himself, or any other person, recognises as John Smith is not that which knows. It is precisely this complex of known or knowable objects, or some aspect thereof. But the knowing subject, as distinct from the known objects, does not have the characteristics of John Smith. Indeed, it does not have any physical, emotional, or ideational characteristics at all; it is knowing pure and simple, and this is that mysterious identity which can neither be made an object of knowledge nor imagined as permanently annihilated.'

The Space Within The Heart

Aubrey Menen, the son of an Indian father and an Irish mother, and a distinguished man of letters, has described his personal experiences of stripping the ego of its skins and of finding the Self. Alan Watts shocked some of his more conventional readers in his autobiography. Aubrey Menen did the same in *The Space Within the Heart* (Hamish Hamilton), a title taken from the *Upanishads*. Both these writers see in sensual pleasures nothing inimical to the mystical life. In this view Mr. Menen believes he has the backing of the *Upanishads*. He says that the *Upanishads* contradicted the *Vedas*, but 'by some chance they got bound up with them.' 'Some keen brains' set about 'reconciling the two' and 'six whole schools of Hindu philosophy arose, one of which was the Vedanta'. 'In this process the text of the *Upanishads* was often distorted and sometimes downright faked.' He also says: 'The philosophers of the *Upanishads*, after having led the reader into the very depths of his being, with shattering results to all his dearest beliefs, advise him to get up and go and enjoy himself like anybody else, with, they specify, horses, chariots, food and women. The verses in which this is said are as coarse as a hearty laugh and a slap on the back. How people manage to find God in such a book I cannot say, but I think it may be that they have a natural refinement which puts things decently straight.'

Mr. Menen advises: 'The Western reader should begin with the seventh section of the eighth chapter of the *Chandogya Upanishad*. Then he should shut himself alone in some quiet place, and think.'

Aubrey Menen himself read the *Upanishads* and sat down to think in a room at the centre of the Thieves' Quarter in Rome. One by one he stripped away the conditioned skins of his ego – beliefs, attitudes, fears, hopes, loves, hates, social roles, and so on.

'As the *Upanishads* describe it,' he tells us, 'the process is like peeling an onion. One by one, you strip away those parts of your personality which consist of the things that you do because the world taught you to do them, or made you do them. Layer by layer – your parents' advice, your schooling, your job, your social position – all go. These are not you. Now it is the turn of your most intimate affairs, your secret hopes, your fears, your dreams. They, too, come from outside you, and they go. At last you come to your loves, your sexual life with others. You cling to those. Surely they are truly your own?

'But they go . . . '

'Then,' he concludes, 'one evening, after a long day of thought in which I did not leave my room even to eat, I saw that everything had gone and there was no more to discard. I looked for my true self.

'Now, if you peel an onion of all its layers, you find nothing. And that is exactly what I found.

'I put away the *Upanishads*, for they had achieved their purpose. I had arrived at the very core of my being. The *Upanishads*, which are written in poetry, call it the space within the heart.'

And what does it feel like to know the Self?

'There is, let me hasten to add, no ethereal blue light. There is, indeed, some sort of feeling, and it is much deeper than "I think, therefore I am". Sometimes I described it to myself as a sort of disembodied laughter, but in doing so I was merely a writer making a phrase about something which no phrase can describe.'

In this chapter we have seen how various experts have gone about dispelling the illusion of possessing an ego-self. Mostly they rely on an analytical approach and on the power of the intellect to peel away one by one the ego's conditioned skins. However, so deeply entrenched is most Westerner's sense of a 'skin-encapsulated ego' that to dissolve it requires the aid of other techniques of meditative awareness, such as following the breath or repeating a *mantra*. These methods, too, aim at uncovering the Self beyond the ego.

9

Love Finds the Way

1. *Meditate in a place where distractions of noises, voices, and so on are within your tolerance level.*
2. *Sit motionless, poised, and comfortable.*
3. *Breathe quietly, gently, smoothly, and rhythmically. Breathe through the nostrils and down into the abdomen.*
4. *Sustain loving attention as the subject of meditation. This may be aroused by adoration of God, the Absolute, or some revered figure; by selfless love of a man, woman, or child; by openness to the mystery and wonder of Being; by contemplation of Nature or something of ego-dissolving beauty; and so on.*
5. *Observe a relaxed and passive attitude towards distractions, including thoughts and images that disrupt loving attention. Even thoughts and images associated with that which is loved should be treated as distractions and gone beyond to experience pure being.*

Love, devotion, and aspiration, when strong and pure, find ways of meditation to use, as water finds folds in the earth into which to flow. The method of meditation used feels to the meditator as natural as breathing. Awareness of breathing itself may be one of the 'neutral' methods – available to people of all temperaments and all credal affiliations – into which devotional meditation may flow; but more often the methods favoured are repetition, aloud or silently, of sacred words, such as the name of God or short prayers, gazing upon or visualising a symbol of deep meaningfulness to the meditator, and, most frequently of all, contemplative prayer, a method that specifically belongs to devotional meditation and therefore to this chapter. Contemplative prayer may begin with words and images, but as it deepens it goes beyond them to the experience of pure awareness.

The love of a man for a woman, a woman for a man, of a mother or father for a child, or of an artist for his art can at its finest attain the level of contemplation. There is too the love of nature, which overlaps or borders on the religious, as with William Wordsworth and Richard Jeffries. We are concerned here mainly with devotional meditation as a mystical 'way' or Yoga, as found in the spiritual training of the major religions. It is the main form of meditation in the theistic religions of Judaism, Christianity, and Islam, and in the Bhakti sects in Hinduism, in which the Divine is worshipped in a personalised form.

In this chapter we will first look at the power of love to transform consciousness, then at the Indian Hindu tradition of Bhakti, then at Christian contemplative prayer, followed by the Sufi treatment of devotional love, and we conclude with brief mention of the contemplative love of Nature.

The Power of Love

The power of love to elevate, conquer, and transform has been lauded in the literature of every major religion. It is, too, the fire which supplies the energy and light for contemplatives seeking knowledge of God or Reality.

'For he who fights with love will win the battle,' says the *Tao Te Ching*, 67. 'He who defends with love will be secure. Heaven will save him and protect him with love.'

Love or loving-kindness (*Metta*) is the first of the Four Brahma Viharas or Sublime States of Consciousness which Buddhists are encouraged to cultivate, and Compassion is the second. The third and fourth are Joy and Equanimity respectively. In the Buddhist *Itivuttaka* it is written: 'All the means that can be used as bases for right action are not worth the sixteenth part of the emancipation of the heart through love. This takes all others up into itself, outshining them in glory. Just as whatsoever stars there be, their radiance avails not the sixteenth part of the radiance of the moon, just as the sun, mounting up into a clear and cloudless sky, overwhelms all darkness in the realms of space . . . so all means towards right action avail not the sixteenth part of the emancipation of the heart through love.' In meditation, Buddhists are instructed to radiate love and compassion to every quarter of the world. The effect is an expansion of consciousness.

The anonymous author of *The Cloud of Unknowing*, a fourteenth-century Christian treatise, wrote:

'All reasonable creatures, angel and man, have in them, each one by himself, one principal working power, the which is called a knowing power, and another principal working power, the which is called a loving power. Of the which two powers, to the first, the which is a knowing power, God who is the maker of them is evermore incomprehensible; but to the second, the which is the loving power, he is, in every man diversely, all comprehensible to the full. Insomuch that one loving soul alone in itself, by virtue of love, may comprehend in itself him who is sufficient to the full – and much more, without comparison – to fill all the souls and angels that may be. And this is the endless marvellous miracle of love, the working of which shall never have end, for ever shall he do it, and never shall he cease for to do it.

'See, whoso by grace see may; for the feeling of this is endless bliss, and the contrary is endless pain.'

Rabindranath Tagore (1861–1941), the Indian poet and writer, wrote in *Sadhana* (Macmillan) of what *The Cloud of Unknowing* called the 'knowing power' of love: 'Intellectual knowledge is partial, because our intellect is an instrument, it is only a part of us, it can give us information about things which can be divided and analysed, and whose properties can be classified, part by part. But Brahmā is perfect, and knowledge which is partial can never be a knowledge of him.

'But he can be known by joy, by love. For joy is knowledge in its completeness, it is knowing by our whole being. Intellect sets us apart from the things to be known, but love knows its object by fusion. Such knowledge is immediate and admits no doubt. It is the same as knowing our own selves, only more so.

'Therefore, as the *Upanishads* say, mind can never know

Brahmā, words can never describe him; he can only be known by our soul, by her joy in him, by her love. Or, in other words, we can only come into relation with him by union – union of our whole being. We must be one with our Father, we must be perfect as he is.'

Tagore is describing love as a mystical way or Yoga in the Hindu tradition. The other major religions also speak of love as a path to mystical union with God or with Being. The gospel of St. John described the Christian approach: 'Let us love one another: for love is of God; but every one that loveth is born of God and knoweth God. He that loveth not knoweth not God; for God is love.'

Henri Bergson (1859–1941), philosopher of the *elan vital*, wrote: 'God is love and the end of love: this is the whole contribution of mysticism. The mystic will never tire of speaking of this twofold love. His descriptions are without end, because he seeks to describe the indescribable. But he is certain on one point: that divine love is not something belonging to God: it is God himself.'

Love as meditation involves emptying the mind of all content except *loving*, which acts as a purificatory flame. St. John of the Cross (1542–91), said that love sets the soul on fire and destroys all in it that is not love. Abu 'abd Allah al-Quarashi, a Sufi, put it: 'Love means giving all you have to Him who you love, so that nothing remains to you of your own.' Here we have yet another way of stripping the ego of its skins.

BHAKTI YOGA

Bhakti is the Hindu term for religious devotion. Brahman, the all-pervading universal spirit of Hindu philosophy and metaphysics, is too dry and intellectual a concept for the devotional Bhaktas, whose love and adoration centres on divine figures as representatives of the Supreme Being. In particular, Bhakti worship has centred on personal devotion to Vishnu and Shiva (and their avatars or incarnations), who with Brahmā make up the Hindu Trinity, or three aspects of Brahman. Shiva destroys, but in the interests of regeneration; Brahmā creates; and Vishnu preserves. Devotion to Vishnu (Vaishnavism) often centres on

Vishnu's manifestations as Rama and Krishna. Mahatma Gandhi's last words, following his assassination, were 'Rama, Rama'. Krishna's adventures and amours are related in Indian epic poetry, and he is the spokesman, teaching the Yogas, in the *Bhagavad Gita*.

Bhakti Yoga, the path of adoration and religious love, is the devotional school of Hinduism. Its popularity with the Indian masses is understandable. The paths of Karma Yoga, or religious service, and of Jnana, or knowledge, are limited by caste and by education respectively; whereas the Bhakti way is open to everyone with the necessary feelings of adoration and worship. It is a Yoga open to the illiterate as well as the literate, and to people of low caste as well as of high caste. For a time the Bhakti school was opposed by the Brahmins, the priestly caste, because it ignored caste divisions and traditional religious ceremonies. The Bhakti movement, with its devotional fervour, has tended to be a law unto itself. The spirit of independence is strong in the Bauls of Bengal. Baul means 'madcap' and refers to their freedom from doctrinal ties. One of their songs says: 'In love there is no separation, but a meeting of hearts forever. So I rejoice in song and I dance with each and all. That is why, brother, I became a madcap Baul.'

Hinduism contains within its elastic boundaries – if, indeed, it can be said to have boundaries at all – polytheism and monotheism, pantheism, deism, theism, and atheism. With the characteristic openness of Hinduism, Bhakti devotion is quite willing to include the Buddha and Christ among the incarnations worthy of worship. Hinduism is generous in such matters: there are no doctrinal rigidities. This openness is well expressed in the teachings of Ramakrishna (1834–1866), one of the great figures of the Bhakti school. He believed that devotion was the best path for the modern age. Biographies of him have been written by Romain Rolland and Christopher Isherwood. He pronounced that all religions are paths to the one Truth. 'It is one and the same avatar who has plunged into the ocean of life and appears now as Krishna, now as Christ. Avatars – such as Rama, Krishna, Buddha, Christ are related to the absolute Brahman as single waves to the whole ocean.' He also said: 'I have tried all religions – Hinduism, Mohammadism, and Christianity – and I have found that all by different roads seek the same God.'

Ramakrishna's most famous disciple, Swami Vivekananda (1862–1902), taught a synthesis of several Yogas – Bhakti, Jnana, Raja, and so on – and carried to America the philosophy of Advaita Vedanta (non-duality, the oneness of the universe) based on the message of the *Upanishads*. He called on his countrymen to deal with the social evils that abounded in India.

Later, Sri Aurobindo Ghose (1872–1950) also taught an integral Yoga based on a synthesis of several paths. His writings, like those of Vivekananda, have been influential. A 'Yoga town' called Auroville was established in India as a place for the study and practice of Aurobindo's teachings. His successor as a teacher was a Frenchwoman, known simply as The Mother, who had worked closely with him. Among her writings is the following description of meditation based on pure aspiration. It has similarities to Christian contemplative prayer as will shortly be shown.

Meditation as Naked Aspiration

'There is (a) kind of meditation which consists in being as quiet as one can be, but without trying to stop all thoughts, for there are thoughts that are purely mechanical and if you try to stop these, you will need years and besides you may not be sure of the result; instead of that you gather together the whole of your consciousness and remain as quiet and peaceful as possible, you detach yourself from the external things as though they do not interest you at all, and all on a sudden you kindle that flame of aspiration and throw into it everything that comes to you so that the flame may rise more and more, more and more; you identify yourself with it and you go up to the extreme point of your consciousness and aspiration, thinking of nothing else – simply, an aspiration that mounts, mounts, mounts, without thinking a minute of the result, of what may happen and especially of what may not happen and above all not to have the desire for something to happen to you – simply, the joy of an aspiration that mounts and mounts and mounts, intensifying itself more and more in a constant concentration.

'And there I can assure you that what happens is the best that can happen. That is to say it is the maximum of your possibilities that is realised when you do that. These possibilities may be very different according to individuals. But then all this care about trying to be silent, going behind the appearances, calling a force that answers, waiting for an answer to your questions, all that vanishes like an unreal vapour. And if you succeed in living consciously in this flame, in this column of mounting aspiration, you will see that even if you do not have an immediate result, after a time something will come to you.' (*Bulletin*, August 1964, Sri Aurobindo Society, Pondicherry.)

Contemplative Prayer

Meditation as a pure flame of aspiration is of similar kind to Christian contemplative prayer in its wordless and imageless higher stages. The poet Rilke defined prayer as a direction of the heart. A medieval English mystic called it 'naught else but a yearning of the soul'. 'Look that nothing live in thy working mind but a naked intent stretching unto God,' wrote the anonymous author of the *Epistle of Privy Counsel*. And the same writer, in *The Cloud of Unknowing*, advises: 'Strike that thick cloud of unknowing with the sharp dart of longing love, and on no account think of giving up.' Here we have cogent definitions of contemplative prayer.

The word 'prayer' may have embarrassing associations for some readers for whom prayer means asking God publicly or privately for some favour or at any rate to intervene in some manner in the course of events, or thanking Him for favours granted. Contemplative prayer is not of this kind, but resembles the approach of Eastern meditation, in which the meditator does not consider the immediate rewards of prayer.

Spoken prayers have their place in religious ritual and in private devotions, but contemplative prayer is essentially a 'prayer of the heart'.

Prayer of the Heart

'In meditation, go deep in the heart,' says Lao Tzu, *Tao Te Ching*, 8. The heart is a recurring metaphor and symbol in the meditation of religious adoration. According to the *Upanishads*, the Self is found in 'the space within the heart'. 'God is in thy heart, yet thou searchest for him in the wilderness,' says *The Granth*, the 'holy book' of the Sikhs. Contemplative prayer is an attentiveness of the heart.

'Why do we pray so much with our lips and so little with the heart?' asked the Abbé Grou in *L'Ecole de Jesus Christ*, written in the late nineteenth century. 'Why do we not draw our prayers from this source, instead of having recourse to our memory and our lips?' The Abbé Grou wrote that prayer 'is wholly a spiritual act, directed to Him who is the Spirit of spirits, the Spirit who sees all things and who is, as St. Augustine says, more intimately present to our soul than its deepest of depths. If we add to what is of the essence of prayer certain bodily postures, words, external marks of devotion: all these of themselves mean nothing, and are only pleasing to God in as much as they express the sentiments of the soul. It is, properly speaking, the *heart* that prays; it is to the voice of the heart that God lends an attentive ear. Whosoever speaks of the heart means that which is most spiritual within us. It is indeed noteworthy that in Holy Scripture prayer is always attributed to the heart; it is moreover the heart that God teaches and it is the heart, when instructed how to pray, that afterwards enlightens the understanding.'

The form of prayer which the Abbé Grou praises as the highest is the Prayer of Quiet which is naked aspiration or stretching of the heart towards God. 'The heart is full of thoughts of God, which it is unable to express clearly, and which are so spiritual that they escape its knowledge, but they are not unknown to God. This prayer so empty of all images, and seemingly inactive, is yet so active that it is, as far as it can be so in this life, pure adoration in spirit and in truth: the adoration that is really worthy of God where the soul is united to him in its very depth, the created intelligence to the uncreated intelligence, without the medium of the imagination or of the reasoning powers, or anything beyond a very simple attention of the understanding, and an equally simple application of the will. This is what is called the prayer of silence, the prayer of quiet, of simple contemplation . . .'

Dom Cuthbert Butler, a twentieth-century Benedictine monk, also described the prayer of simplicity and loving attention: 'One sets oneself to pray, say for the regulation half hour; empties the mind of all images, ideas, concepts – this is commonly done without much difficulty.

'Fixes the soul in loving attention on God, without express or distinct ideas of Him, beyond the vague incomprehensible idea of His Godhead; makes no particular acts but a general actuation of love, without sensible devotion or emotional feelings: a sort of blind and dumb act of the will or of the soul itself. This lasts a few minutes, then fades away, and either a blank or distractions supervene: when recognised, the will again fixes the mind in "loving attention" for a time. The period of prayer is thus passed in such alternations, a few minutes each, the bouts of loving attention being, in favourable conditions, more prolonged than the bouts of distraction.' (*Western Mysticism*, Constable.)

The passage just quoted makes very clear how Christian contemplative prayer functions in the ways that were described in Chapter 3 – effortless attention alternating with stretches of pure awareness or distractions which, once conscious, become the signal to switch back to meditative attention.

Stages of Prayer

The type of prayer we are discussing has clear correspondences with the meditation of Hinduism, Buddhism, Taoism, and other Eastern systems. In Christian literature prayers and meditations are called 'spiritual exercises' or 'spiritual training', the Eastern name for which is Yoga. But the stages of Christian prayer have been less clearly delineated than those of Eastern meditation. Individual Christian mystics have described the 'ascent' to mystical consciousness, but Christianity has not had a systematiser of the calibre of Patanjali, who codified the techniques of Yogic meditation. The Eastern religions are esoteric psychologies and investigate the nuances of states of consciousness in remarkable detail. Sanskrit and Pali, the two languages in which Hindu and Buddhist scriptures are written, are said to have more terms describing states of consciousness than all the modern languages combined, as pointed out earlier. Christian writers do not always use the same terms to describe the stages or 'degrees' (as they are sometimes called) of prayer, and when they do they sometimes use the terms in an individual manner. But the stages do have essential features that correspond with those of the Eastern mystical psychologies. Whatever the terms used, Christian contemplation, like its Eastern counterparts, aims to lead the meditator to the profound silence and illumination of unitary consciousness. Even though Christian theologians and those of other religions interpret mystical consciousness according to their own doctrines, even a cursory study of the characteristics of the experience *per se* shows that it is something shared by men and women, of many religions, and of none.

F. C. Happold, in his *Mysticism: a Study and an Anthology* (Penguin Books) says: 'There is much variation in the ways the degrees of prayer are described, and it is easy to become confused.' He simplifies by reducing them to the three stages of Recollection, Quiet, and Contemplation proper. Here he is following the approach of Evelyn Underhill in her famous study *Mysticism* (Methuen). This suits us nicely because it corresponds well with the stages of meditation which we described as having universal validity in Chapter 3.

Recollection corresponds to Buddhist mindfulness and to the preliminary stages of sense-withdrawal (*pratyahara*) and concentration (*dharana*) in Raja Yoga. It is the stage of sitting still, of ignoring the sense impressions reaching the meditator from external objects, of turning the attention inwards and gathering together (collecting) the energies of consciousness. The similarity to Yogic *dharana* is well brought out by Jakob Boehme (1575–1624), the German cobbler mystic, who instructed: 'Cease from thine own activity, fix thine eye upon one point . . . Gather in all thy thoughts and by faith press into the Centre . . . Be silent before the Lord, sitting alone with Him in thy inmost and most hidden cell, thy inward being centrally united in itself, and attending His will in the patience of hope.'

In the early stage of contemplative prayer, words and images may be used. If words are used, it will usually be repetition of a single sacred word or a short prayer so as to induce mental calm and recollection. Prayer with words gives way to wordless prayer. Similarly, a visual aid – an object with symbolic meaning – may be gazed upon or visualised; but again, as the contemplation deepens, the content becomes formless and only the 'naked intent' or loving remains, though not named or thought about.

The Prayer of Quiet corresponds to Yogic and Buddhist *dhyana* or meditation. It arises naturally out of sustained Recollection and in its quietude meditation becomes effortless. The mind is receptive to and open to the Divine. The grip of the ego-self is loosened. There are feelings of joy and peace.

Evelyn Underhill in *Mysticism* wrote of the transition from Recollection to Quiet: 'As Recollection becomes deeper, the self slides into a certain dim yet vivid consciousness of the Infinite. The door tight shut on the sensual world, it becomes aware that it is immersed in a more real world which it cannot define. It rests quietly in this awareness: quite silent, utterly at peace . . . Here, in this complete cessation of man's proud effort to do somewhat of himself, Humility, who rules the Fourth Degree of Love, begins to be known in her paradoxical beauty and power. Consciousness loses to find, and dies that it may live.' And Dr. Happold, in his more recent study of mysticism, says of the stage of Quiet: 'The self is content to rest in a new level of vivid awareness, marked by deep peace and living stillness . . . There is still a consciousness of selfhood, but the very meaning of I, Me, Mine, has been somehow transformed.'

St. Teresa of Avila (1515–82) wrote detailed accounts of the stages of contemplative prayer and of mystical experience. Her description of the Prayer of Quiet in *The Way of Perfection* was based on her experience of it. The following is a part of what she says:

'It is like the suspension of all internal and external powers. The eternal man . . . does not wish to make the slightest movement but rests, like one who has almost reached the end of his journey, that he may resume his journey with redoubled strength . . . The soul is so happy to find herself near the fountain that she is satisfied even without drinking. She seems to have no more to desire. The faculties are at peace and do not wish to move . . . However, the faculties are not so lost that they cannot think of Him whom they are near. Two of them are free. The will alone is held captive . . . The understanding desires to know but one thing, and the memory to remember only one. They both see that only one thing is necessary, and everything else disturbs it . . . I think, therefore, that since the soul is so completely happy in this prayer of quiet, the will must be united, during most of the time, with Him who alone can satisfy it.'

During the stage of Quiet, contemplation becomes effortless – a smooth flow of attention that may lead to the highest stage of union with the Divine. St. Teresa likened the stages to watering a garden. First the water has to be drawn from the well by hand; later there is the assistance of a windlass and bucket; then it is as though a river irrigates the garden, 'for it is God who does everything'; and in the final union the watering of the garden may be left to God's rain. Thus contemplation becomes progressively less a doing and its final stages are effortless.

Jan van Ruysbroeck (1293–1381), the Flemish mystic, described the stage of union as 'a melting and dying into the Essential Nudity'. Buddhists speak of the Void (*sunyata*) or Emptiness, and Christian mystics who have experienced mystical consciousness use similar expressions. The characteristics of unitary consciousness were discussed earlier and need not be gone into again. Ruysbroeck added: 'here there is nought but an eternal rest in the fruitive embrace of an outpouring Love'.

Prayer and Happier Living

Dame Julian of Norwich (c. 1342–1420), an English Benedictine nun, summed up the goal of contemplative prayer when she said: 'Prayer oneth the soul with God.' This could be said to be the goal of all mystical meditation, though some mystics prefer to speak of a non-personal Absolute, Being, Cosmic Consciousness, and so on, rather than of God.

However, prayer of the kind we have been discussing need not be reserved only for devout contemplatives. The psycho-physiological benefits derived from the practice of meditation described in Chapter 2 also result from the practice of contemplative prayer and do not depend on the attainment of advanced stages of mystical consciousness.

F. C. Happold, in *Prayer and Meditation* (Penguin Books), says that prayer has for its highest goal 'union with the divine' but at a more easily realised level 'prayer becomes an activity in which one may deliberately engage in order that one may lead a happier, fuller and healthier life'. This applies to meditation in general.

Dr Happold sees prayer as 'a way whereby the division between the conscious and the unconscious is overcome'. This makes it a psychotherapy, which meditation has proved itself to be in many cases. However, prayer and meditation should not be viewed as substitutes for medical treatment of psychotic conditions.

Some practitioners of contemplative prayer experience a welling up of great energy, whose separate physical, mental, and spiritual components are difficult to distinguish. They have the feeling that contact has been made with some immeasurable source of energy rooted deep within themselves yet belonging to the essential nature of the cosmos. Doubtless this is due in part to the release of stress from body and mind, and also to contact with the energies of the unconscious. But religious persons also speak of the infusion of the divine spirit.

Lama Anagarika Govinda, in an article published in *The Middle Way*, August 1964, wrote: 'Prayer becomes a source of strength and certainty and not a mere sedative and tranquilliser. The inner peace that comes from prayer is due to the establishment of a balance between the forces of our individual consciousness and the vast potentialities of our depth consciousness, in which the experience of a beginningless past are stored and through which we participate in that greater life that encompasses the universe and connects us with every living being . . . Prayer turns our conscious mind inwards and transforms the potential forces of the depths into active ones.'

Prayer for the Buddhists, though they do not have the concept of a personal God, is the act of opening up the mind and making it receptive that we have described in the practice of Christian contemplative prayer. 'Prayer is an act of opening heart and mind,' says Lama Govinda, 'and while we open ourselves we not only allow the light to enter, but we make the first breach in the walls of our self-created prison, which separates us from our fellow beings. Thus, in the same measure in which the light streams in and makes us recognise our true universal nature which connects us with all that exists in the infinity of space and time, our love and compassion for all living and suffering beings wells up and streams from us like a mighty current that embraces the whole world. In this way prayer becomes an act of devotion in a twofold way: to the forces of light as well as to our fellow beings. The forces of light are not, however, an abstract ideal but a living reality, embodied in those great leaders of humanity, whom we venerate as Enlightened Ones.'

The poet Samuel Taylor Coleridge (1772–1834) expressed the nature of prayer brilliantly in one short sentence: 'Prayer is the effort to live in the spirit of the whole.' See also Henry Vaughan (1622–95): 'Prayer is the world in tune.'

Prayer as That Which Is Sought

Mystics of various creeds have expressed the idea that the act of praying is itself the goal of the mystical quest. Walter Hilton, an Englishman who died in 1396 and believed that mystical experience was potentially within reach of everyone, said: 'He it is that desireth in thee, and He it is that is desired.' And Rabbi Pinhas of Korez wrote: 'The people think that they pray before God. But it is not so. For the prayer itself is the essence of the Godhead.' In similar vein, members of the Soto sect of Zen, one of the two main schools, believe that zazen (sitting meditation) is in itself the goal of meditation. But nowhere is this view more effectively expressed than in the following poem by the Sufi Jalal al-Din Rumi, who died in 1273:

> One night a certain man cried 'Allah!' till his lips grew sweet
>   with praising Him.
> The Devil said, 'O man of many words, where is the response
>   "Here am I" to all this "Allah"?
> Not a single response is coming from the Throne; how long
>   will you say "Allah" with grim face?'
> He was broken-hearted and lay down to sleep: in a dream he
>   saw Khadir amidst the verdure,
> Who said, 'Hark, you have held back from praising God:
>   why do you repent of calling unto Him?'
> He answered, 'No "Here am I" is coming to me in response:
>   I fear that I am turned away from the Door.'

> *Said Khadir, 'Nay; God saith: "That 'Allah' of thine is My*
> *'Here am I', and that supplication and grief*
> *And ardour of thine is My messenger to thee. Thy fear and*
> *love are the noose to catch my favour:*
> *Beneath every 'O Lord' of thine is many a 'Here am I' from*
> *Me."* [2]

Sufi Ecstasy

The Sufis first appeared, mainly in Persia, during the eighth and ninth centuries AD. They were desert wanderers, who dressed in clothing made from coarse wool called 'suf' in Arabic – hence their name. Sufism is the mystical heart of Islam, though claiming to be the essence of all religions. It shows the characteristics of all mysticism, but places major emphasis on devotional love and the surrender of the ego-self to God. The Sufis meditate and cultivate spiritual growth so as to find that which they call the 'One Real'.

R. A. Nicholson, in *Mystics of Islam* (Routledge and Kegan Paul), says: 'It (Sufism) is this: that God should make thee die to thyself and should make thee live in Him.' The theme is familiar. Merging one's life with that of God or the Absolute has its parallels in other traditions that feature in this book. It is the 'That thou art' (*tat twam asi*) of the Hindus, union with the Tao, realising one's Buddha-nature, and St. Paul's 'I live; yet not I, but Christ liveth in me.'

The Sufis provide a concise summary of the technique of stripping the ego of its skins which I call the Onion Game and which is the subject of Chapter 8. (See the Sufic text quoted on page 123 for a summary of this method.)

When the last skin has been discarded and the ego has vanished, the nothingness that remains is the Self beyond the ego, a state of consciousness impossible to describe except by negations; i.e. it is not this, and it is not that. Mahmud Shabistari, a Sufi teacher, wrote: 'Go you, sweep out the dwelling-room of your heart, prepare it to be the abode and home of the Beloved: when you go out He will come in. Within you, when you are free from self, He will show His beauty. When you and your real self become pure from all defilement, there remains no distinction among things, the known and the Knower are all one.'

The obstacles to knowing the real Self and essence have to be removed. The power of love sustains this inner work. The ascent to the state called 'universal man' is through modalities of consciousness (*hals*) which have their parallel stages of behaviour (*moqams*). The final stage of awareness is what is called Cosmic Consciousness in various cultures. The Sufi uncovers a cosmic self and feels linked with all mankind in a way that transcends cultural and credal differences.

Like Zen, Sufism has a flavour all its own. Sufis regard the dogmas of religions – heaven and hell, for example – as allegories. They may marry and follow trades and professions, practising their spiritual exercises secretly at home. The goal of surrender to God does not preclude appreciation of the world; but the senses have to be purified so that the world is seen as it really is. A well-known line by William Blake (1757–1827) comes to mind: 'If the doors of perception were cleansed, everything would appear to man as it is, infinite.' Like other mystics, the Sufi aims to discover what he is by direct knowledge. Love and gnosis are the cornerstones of the system. The way is that of merging in love and devotion with God. The 'letting go' or 'melting away' in ecstatic union is called *fana.*

Sufi Poetry

The distinct flavour of Sufism is captured in its poetry. Only St. John of the Cross is of comparable stature among Christian poet-mystics. Most of the Sufi poets are Persians. They do not hesitate to use the language and imagery of the senses, in particular love between the sexes and intoxication with wine (despite the Islamic prohibition on alcohol). The Sufi poets praise the one God (called 'the Beloved' or 'the Friend'), absolute beauty, and divine love. Though the beauty of the world and the enjoyment of the senses are praised, the poets do not lose sight of their source.

Thus Jami (1414–92) writes:

> *The Loved One's rose-parterre I went to see,*
> *That beauty's Torch espied me, and, quoth He,*

> '*I am the tree; these flowers My offshoots are,*
> *Let not these offshoots hide from thee the tree.*'

Jalal al-Din Rumi (died 1273), who was quoted above, is acknowledged to be the greatest of the Sufi poets. He taught that the true Self should not be identified with the ego conditioned by society and environment, and that the real essence of man is the product of the universe in evolution. Those persons whose approach to mysticism is based on evolution to higher states of consciousness will find much to attract them in Sufism.

For Rumi, love is the energy behind the evolution of human consciousness. It is a dynamic force producing all worthwhile development and creativity in human beings. It arises when the conventional, phenomenal ego lets go.

> *Love is as obvious as the sun and moon in the world,*
> *With such clarity and obviousness why search for proof?*

Rumi founded the famous order of the Mevlevi or Whirling Dervishes. The dervishes dance in a circle and gradually speed up their rotations until they fall into a trance of ecstasy. Here again, as in the other methods of this book, the special quality of attention makes this an exercise in meditation. Traditionally, the instrument used for the dance has been the Persian reed flute, made the symbol of a beautiful poem by Rumi called *The Song of the Reed*. The poem is about the call to union with God.

> *Hearken to this Reed forlorn*
> *Breathing, ever since 'twas torn*
> *From its rusty bed, a strain*
> *Of impassioned love and pain.*
>
> *The secret of my song, though new,*
> *None can see and none can hear.*
> *Oh, for a friend to know the sign*
> *And mingle all his soul with mine!*
>
> *'Tis the flame of love that fired me,*
> *'Tis the wine of love inspired me.*
> *Wouldst thou learn how loves bleed,*
> *Hearken, hearken to the Reed!*

Sufi Methods

Sufi methods of meditation and spiritual training have been closely shielded, but include those that one would expect from a form of mysticism based on devotional love: prayer, aloud and silent, the repetition of the name of God (*dhikr*), gazing upon mystical diagrams, music and dancing, and so on. However, most of the methods described in the chapters of this book are used by the Sufis, including regulation of the breath and mindfulness of breathing.

Love of Nature

Communion with Nature, even when conventional religious belief may not be present, may take on the quality and depth of a prayer of the heart.

William Wordsworth (1770–1850), in his *Tintern Abbey* poem, wrote:

> *'And I have felt*
> *A presence that disturbs me with the joy*
> *Of elevated thoughts; a sense sublime*
> *Of something far more deeply interfused,*
> *Whose dwelling is the light of setting suns,*
> *And the round ocean and the living air,*
> *And the blue sky, and in the mind of man:*
> *A motion and a spirit, that impels*
> *All thinking things, all objects of all thought,*
> *And rolls through all things. Thereafter am I still*
> *A lover of the meadows and the woods,*
> *And mountains; and of all that we behold*
> *From this green earth; of all the mighty world*
> *Of eye, and ear – both what they half create,*
> *And what perceive . . .*

A second example, in prose this time, comes from Richard Jefferies (1848–87), the English naturalist and nature mystic. Though an atheist, he was able to make contemplation of Nature a prayer: an aspiration of his whole being of the kind we gave as a meditation earlier in this chapter. His objection to a personal God

as an 'invisible idol' is familiar enough today in the theology of
the Christian existentialists. In *The Story of My Heart*, Jefferies
wrote:

'I was utterly alone with the sun and the earth. Lying
down on the grass, I spoke in my soul to the earth, the sun,
the air, and the distant sea far beyond sight. I thought of the
earth's firmness – I felt it bear me up; through the grassy
couch there came an influence as if I could feel the great
earth speaking to me. I thought of the wandering air – its
pureness, which is its beauty; the air touched me and gave
me something of itself. I spoke to the sea; though so far, in
my mind I saw it, green at the rim of the earth and blue in
deeper ocean . . . I turned to the blue heaven over, gazing
into its depth, inhaling its exquisite colour and sweetness.
The rich blue of the unattainable flower of the sky drew my
soul towards it, and there it rested, for pure colour is rest of
heart. By all these I prayed . . . Then, returning, I prayed by
the sweet thyme, whose little flowers I touched with my
hand; by the slender grass; by the crumble of dry chalky
earth I took up and let fall through my fingers. Touching the
crumble of earth, the blade of grass, the thyme flower,
breathing the earth-encircling air, thinking of the sea and
the sky, holding out my hand for the sunbeams to touch it,
prone on the sward in token of deep reverence, thus I
prayed . . .[2]

10

Say the Word

1. *Meditate in a place where distractions of noises, voices, and so on are within your tolerance level.*
2. *Sit motionless, poised, and comfortable.*
3. *Breathe quietly, gently, smoothly, and rhythmically. Breathe through the nostrils and down into the abdomen.*
4. *Repeat a word or sound aloud or mentally. Silent, inward repetition is the more subtle practice. The word may have sacred or contemplative associations, be neutral, or have no meaning.*
5. *Observe a relaxed and passive attitude towards distractions, including thoughts and images that flit in and out of the mind. Each time you become conscious that your attention has wandered from the word or sound, bring its repetition back into awareness again. Do this as many times as is necessary, maintaining the relaxed and passive attitude.*

The method with which we are concerned in this chapter is that of repeating a word, phrase, or sound so as to bring the beauty of meditative serenity to the mind and to uncover pure awareness. The Sanskrit name for such a word, phrase, or sound is *mantra*. The practice is common in Hinduism, Buddhism, and Sufism, and it is found in some sections of Christianity. Maharishi Mahesh Yogi's Transcendental Meditation is a more modern form of this meditation which does not depend on religious belief. *Mantra* Yogis believe that the vibrations of *mantra* sounds influence consciousness and that each sound has a particular potency. Devotional meditators are attracted to words of religious significance. However, recent studies by medical scientists show that the repetition of words and sounds, regardless of what they are, induces states of deep psycho-physiological relaxation. The spiritual or occult potency of a word is one thing, and the method itself is another thing. We will be considering both these aspects.

So we see that a *mantra* may be for a meditator sacred, meaningful, neutral, even meaningless. The devotional meditator will be drawn irresistibly to using a sacred word. Another meditator may choose a word such as 'peace' or 'love' that has pleasant associations conducive to contemplation. But every meditator, regardless of whether he has credal affiliations or not, may practise with advantage repetition of a neutral or meaningless *mantra*, trusting to the mechanics of this form of meditation to achieve its effects.

The Power of Words

William James (1842–1910), in his *Varieties of Religious Experience*, wrote of the power of words to trigger experiences of a mystical character:

> 'The simplest rudiment of mystical experience would seem to be that deepened sense of the significance of a maxim or formula which occasionally sweeps over one. "I've heard that said all my life," we exclaim, "but I never realised its full meaning until now." "When a fellow-monk," said Luther, "one day repeated the words of the Creed: 'I believe in the forgiveness of sins', I saw the Scripture in an entirely new light; and straightaway I felt as if I were born anew. It was as if I had found the door of paradise thrown wide open."

> 'This sense of deeper significance is not confined to rational propositions. Single words, and conjunctions of words, effects of light on land and sea, odours and musical sounds, all bring it when the mind is tuned aright. Most of us can remember the strangely moving power of passages in certain poems read when we were young, irrational doorways as they were through which the mystery of fact, the wildness and the pang of life, stole into our hearts and thrilled them. The words have now perhaps become mere polished surfaces for us; but lyric poetry and music are alive and significant only in proportion as they fetch these vague vistas of a life

continuous with our own, beckoning and inviting, yet ever eluding our pursuit. We are alive or dead to the eternal inner message of the arts according as we have kept or lost this mystical susceptibility.'

Simone Weil (1909–43) used to induce mystical ecstasy in herself by repeating the poem *Love* by George Herbert (1593–1633):

> *Love bade me welcome: yet my soul drew back,*
> *Guilty of dust and sin.*
> *But quick-ey'd Love, observing me grow slack*
> *From my first entrance in,*
> *Drew nearer to me, sweetly questioning,*
> *If I lack'd any thing.*
>
> *A guest, I answer'd, worthy to be here:*
> *Love said, You shall be he.*
> *I the unkind, ungrateful? Ah, my dear,*
> *I cannot look on thee.*
> *Love took my hand, and smilingly did reply,*
> *Who made the eyes but I?*
>
> *Truth Lord, but I have marr'd them: let my shame*
> *Go where it doth deserve.*
> *And know you not, says Love, who bore the blame?*
> *My dear, then I will serve.*
> *You must sit down, says Love, and taste my meat:*
> *So I did sit and eat.*

The power of certain words or poetry to evoke altered states of consciousness depends on by chance encounters and discoveries, whereas use of the mantra is systematic. Mantras are sound-forms serving the purposes of meditation, just as yantras (described in Chapter 6) are designs used for visual meditation.

MANTRA YOGA

The use of the mantra is one of the commonest forms of meditation in Hinduism, especially in its devotional schools. The mantra is usually a Sanskrit word or phrase which is believed to have mystical or occult potency. It is repeated so as to alter consciousness, aloud or mentally; the latter is the most subtle use of the mantra.

Sri Aurobindo defined the mantra from the traditional viewpoint: 'a direct and most heightened, an intense and most divinely burdened rhythmic word which embodies an intuitive and revelatory inspiration and ensouls the reality of things and with its truth and with the divine soul-forms of it, the Godheads which are born from the living truth.'

There is in India a tradition of a sacred, mystical word or formula being passed down from guru (teacher) to chela (pupil) for the latter's private use. The pupil treasures his mantra and keeps it secret: for he has been told that revealing it to others would reduce its potency. It was in revolt against this huggermugger attitude that Ramanuja (eleventh century), one of the leading figures in the history of devotional Bhakti Yoga, shouted his mantra from the roof of a temple so that all could share it. The tradition of keeping the mantra secret and private has been continued in Maharishi Mahesh Yogi's Transcendental Meditation, though his method differs from the customary repetition of mantras in important ways.

A school of Yoga – Mantra Yoga – centres on the practice of *japa*, the repetition of mantras. The origins of the practice go back to earliest Indian history and it is mentioned in the *Vedas*, the world's oldest scriptures. There are fourteen kinds of *japa*, but we need here look only at two: voiced repetitions and mental repetitions.

In group practice, where there is a strong devotional element, the mantra is often repeated loudly and sonorously. The chants of the monks in Tantric monasteries are of remarkable sonority, setting up vibrations that are almost earth-shaking. Tantric Yogis believe that the vibrations of voiced mantras are health-enhancing as well as aids to meditation, giving a kind of vibromassage to the body's internal organs. This is particularly so, they say, in intoning the supreme Hindu mantra – OM.

OM (AUM) is the *pranava*, the 'word of glory'. It represents the Absolute. It is the logos. 'In the beginning was the Word.'

OM is the Brahman, the universal spirit or consciousness, and meditation upon it leads to absorption, according to Hindu mysticism. The *Mundaka Upanishad* says: 'OM is the bow, the individual self is the arrow, the spirit is the target. One should then become one with it like an arrow that has penetrated the target.'

OM may be used as a yantra or visual symbol and gazed upon in meditation, or it may be used as a mantra. The AU sound (as in the English 'house') begins at the back of the throat and the sound is then brought gradually forward; the lips are then closed and the sound is completed with a strongly vibrated M in the front of the face, the place voice teachers call 'the mask'.

Andre van Lysebeth, a Belgian teacher of Yoga, in *Yoga Self Taught* (Allen and Unwin), recommends voicing OM resonantly because it gives a vibro-massage to the ductless glands and the organs in the chest cavity and the abdomen, tones the nervous system, and stimulates deep breathing. He supports his views by discussing the work of Dr. Leser-Lasario, a scientist who for twenty-five years studied the effects produced in the human organism by vocal vibrations. He found that vocal vibrations produced during exhalation reach deep-lying tissues and nerve cells, improve circulation, stimulate the pituitary, pineal, thyroid, and other glands, and improve breathing. Another effect is to relax the entire body.

Singing and the recitation of poetry of an incantatory rhythm may be viewed as a kind of Yoga. The effectiveness of music therapy shows that sound vibrations can have healing power.

Indian mantras are often preceded by OM – as in the famous OM MANI PADME HUM, which means 'OM, the jewel in the lotus'.

Followers of the Krishna Consciousness Movement have brought the sound of a Sanskrit chant to the streets of American and European cities – HARE KRISHNA, HARE KRISHNA, KRISHNA, KRISHNA, HARE, HARE, HARE, RAMA, HARE RAMA, RAMA RAMA, HARE HARE. This is chanted in a devotional manner and repeated hundreds of times. Adoration of Krishna belongs to the tradition of Bhakti Yoga, the path of religious devotion.

Nembutsu

Members of the Pure Land sects of Buddhism in Japan make their main spiritual practice repetition of the words 'NAMU-AMIDA-BUTSU' – I surrender myself to Amida Buddha'. This is known as *nembutsu*. *Nem* means 'surrendering to' and *butsu* means 'Buddha'. Amida is the Buddha of Infinite Light. Pure Land, with its simple devotional nature, is known as 'the easy way' in contrast to 'the hard way' of Zen. It is the Japanese equivalent of the Indian devotional path of Bhakti Yoga.

Chanting mantras is central practice also for members of another Japanese Buddhist sect, the Shingon-shu. *Shingon* means 'mantra'.

Suffic Dhikr

Wherever in the world's religions there is a strong devotional movement, there is usually found the practice of repeating sacred words. This is certainly true of the Islamic Sufis. As we showed in Chapter 9, the path they follow is that of adoration of God and union ('passing away' or *fana*) with Him.

The name and attributes of God are used as mantras in the Sufis *dhikr* or *zikr*, meaning 'remembrance' and also 'repetition'. Consciousness is gathered together and the mantra repeated with heartfelt devotion. The first line of the Koran is often used as a mantra – *La ilaha illa'llah* ('There is no God but God'). *Ya hu* (O He) is a favourite of the Dervishes. The meditator sits facing *gibla*, the direction of Mecca, though some orders of Dervishes perform the *dhikr* while dancing in a circle.

The devotional exercise of *dhikr* has a prominent place in Islamic spiritual training and meditation. It had the authoritative sanction of Mohammad. There are two main kinds of practice: *dhikr jali*, which is recited aloud, and *dhikr khafi*, which is performed either in a low voice or mentally. These are the same two main forms of practice as found in Mantra Yoga.

Reciting aloud may lead to silent repetition and going beyond the mantra, with progressive refinement of the kind described by Patanjali and which forms the basis of both age-old types of meditation and new presentations of old methods, as in Transcendental Meditation. This is clearly described in the instruction in *dhikr* given by al-Ghazali (1059–1111), whose reputation as a scholar, philosopher, and theologian earned him the nickname 'the proof of Islam'. The passage has been summarised by D. B. Macdonald and appears in S. M. Zwemer's *A Moslem Seeker After God* (Fleming H. Revell, New York).

'Let the worshipper reduce his heart to a state in which the existence of anything and its non-existence are the same to him. Then let him sit alone in some corner, limiting his religious duties to what is absolutely necessary, and not occupying himself either with reciting the Koran or considering its meaning or with books of religious traditions or with anything of the sort. And let him see to it that nothing save God most High enters his mind. Then, as he sits in solitude, let him not cease saying continuously with his tongue, "Allah, Allah," keeping his thoughts on it. At last he will reach a state when the motion of his tongue will cease, and it will seem as though the word flowed from it. Let him persevere in this until all trace of motion is removed from his tongue, and he finds his heart persevering in the thought. Let him still persevere until the form of the word, its letters and shape, is removed from his heart, and there remains the idea alone, as though clinging to his heart, inseparable from it. So far, all is dependent on his will and choice; but to bring the mercy of God does not stand in his will or choice. He has now laid himself bare to the breathings of that mercy, and nothing remains but to wait what God will open to him, as God has done after this manner to prophets and saints. If he follows the above course, he may be sure that the light of the Real will shine out in his heart.'

There is clear similarity here with the higher forms of Christian contemplative prayer, in which recollection or concentration moves on to effortless meditation.

In some orders both the two main forms of prayer are followed: aloud and mentally. Some Sufi teachers instruct their disciples that the heart has two doors: a fleshly door and a spiritual door. *Dhikr jali* opens the fleshly door and *dhikr khafi* opens the spiritual door.

Breath control is sometimes linked with recitation of the sacred words. In one method the words 'LA ILAHA ILLA 'LLAH'

(There is no God but God), are recited three times on one intake of breath.

However, the main essential in *dhikr* is that the words should be recited 'with the tongue of the heart'. Repeatedly in Sufi instruction and poetry the symbol of the heart crops up. A nineteenth-century Sufi wrote:

'The heart is kept constantly occupied with the idea of the Most High God; it will be filled with awe, love, and respect for Him; and, if the practiser arrives at the power of continuing to effect this when in the company of a crowd, the *zikr* is perfect. If he cannot do this, it is clear that he must continue his efforts. The heart is a subtle part of the human frame, and is apt to wander away after worldly concerns, so that the easier mode of arriving at the proceeding is to compress the breath, and keep the mouth firmly closed with the tongue forced against the lips. The heart is shaped like the cone of a fir-tree; your meditations should be forced upon it, whilst you mentally recite the *zikr*. Let the '*La*' be upward, the '*ilaha*' to the right, and the whole phrase 'LA ILAHA ILLA 'LLAH' be formed upon the fir-cone, and through it pass to all the members of the whole frame, and they feel its warmth. By this means the world and all its attractions disappear from your vision, and you are enabled to behold the excellence of the Most High. Nothing must be allowed to distract your attention from the *zikr*, and ultimately you retain, by its medium, a proper conception of the Tauhid, or Unity of God.

'The cone-shaped heart rests in the left breast and contains the whole truth of man. Indeed, it signifies the 'whole truth'; it comprises the whole of man's existence, within itself, and is a compendium of man; mankind, great and small, are but an extension of it, and it is to humanity what the seed is to the whole tree which it contains within itself: *in fine*, the essence of the whole of God's book and of all His secrets is the heart of man.'

Sufis meditate upon teaching stories. One story delightfully brings out the point that the spirit in which a *mantra* is recited

– 'with the tongue of the heart' – is more important than its correct pronunciation.

A somewhat pedantic dervish was walking one day along a river bank. From an island in midstream could be heard someone repeating the dervish call 'YA HU', but mispronouncing it 'U YA HU'. The listening dervish felt it was his duty to correct his brother, so he hired a boat and rowed to the island. There he found a man wearing a dervish robe, sitting in a reed hut and intoning 'U YA HU'. The first dervish pointed out the error in pronunciation and was thanked. As he began to row back to the river bank, he heard the dervish in the reed hut restart the *dhikr* – but incorrectly as before. After a minute or two the sound faltered and then stopped. A few moments later the dervish in the boat was astounded to see the second dervish stepping briskly towards him over the surface of the water. On reaching the boat, the dervish who could walk on water said: 'Brother, forgive my stupidity, but would you mind telling me again the correct method of making the repetition – I find it difficult to remember it!'

The Jesus Prayer

In some sectors of Christianity the value of repetition of short prayers or of the name of Jesus has been known for centuries. There is Christian contemplative practice that parallels Hindu Mantra Yoga and the Sufi *dhikr*.

Diadochus of Photice (fifth century AD) and John Climacus (seventh century AD) recommended repetition of the name of Jesus. The latter wrote: 'If many words are used in prayer, all sorts of distracting pictures hover in the mind but worship is lost. If little is said or only a single word pronounced, the mind remains concentrated.' And the Russian *The Way of a Pilgrim* says: 'If thou wilt that thy prayer be pure, made up of good things, thou must choose a short one consisting of a few powerful words and repeat it many times.'

Orthodox monks and lay people have for centuries found 'a few powerful words' in the Jesus Prayer – 'Lord Jesus Christ, son of God, have mercy on me', or, slightly shorter, 'Lord Jesus Christ, have mercy on me'. The Jesus Prayer has a long tradition of use in Hesychasm, the system of Christian mysticism developed by the monks of Mount Athos in the fourteenth century.

Repetition of the Jesus Prayer is more closely related to the use of the mantra in the Eastern religions than it is to conventional petitionary prayer. This is made clear in the writings on it contained in the five volumes of the *Philokalia,* a collection of writings by the Christian Fathers of the first millenium, preserved in the monasteries of Mount Athos. The similarity to Mantra Yoga may be seen in the following extracts from a selection *Writings from the Philokalia* (Faber and Faber): 'Sit down alone in silence. Lower your head, shut your eyes, breathe out gently, and imagine yourself looking into your own heart. As you breathe out say, "Lord Jesus Christ, have mercy on me." Say it, moving your lips gently, or simply say it in your mind. Try to put all other thoughts aside. Be calm, be patient and repeat the process very frequently.'

Like the Yogis and the Sufis, the Christian Fathers were aware of the value of linking the repetitions of the prayer with the rhythms of breathing:

'You know, brother, how do we breathe: we breathe the air in and out. On this is based the life of the body, and on this depends its warmth. So, sitting down in your cell, collect your mind, lead it into the path of the breath, along which the air enters in, constrain it to enter the heart together with the inhaled air, and keep it there. Keep it there, but do not leave it silent and idle; instead give it the following prayer: "Lord Jesus Christ, Son of God, have mercy upon me." Let this be its constant occupation, never to be abandoned. For this work, by keeping the mind free from dreaming, renders it unassailable to suggestions of the enemy and leads it to Divine desire and love.'

In Eastern Orthodox writings on the practice of the Jesus Prayer we find all the conditions being fulfilled for the practice of meditation of the kind we describe in this book: a quiet place, poised posture, an object on which the attention dwells effortlessly, and poised passive awareness.

Bishop Ignatius Brianchaninov's essay *On the Prayer of Jesus* (John Watkins) is a valuable short guide to use of the prayer as spiritual training. Bishop Brianchaninov wrote: 'Experience will soon show that in using this method, especially at first, the words should be pronounced with extreme unhurriedness so that the mind may have time to enter the words as into forms.' As always in meditation, patience is shown in bringing the wandering attention back to the object of meditation. 'Try to restore, or more exactly, to enclose your thoughts in the words of the prayer. If on account of its infancy, it wearies and wanders, lead it in again.' The Jesus Prayer is also known as the Prayer of the Heart, when the words are held in the place of the heart. 'It is one thing to pray with attention with the participation of the heart; it is another thing to descend with the mind into the temple of the heart and from there to offer mystical prayer filled with divine grace and power. The second is the result of the first. The attention of the mind during prayer draws the heart into sympathy. With the strengthening of the attention, sympathy of heart and mind is turned into union of heart and mind. Finally when attention makes the prayer its own, the mind descends into the heart for the most profound and sacred service of prayer.'

That this is meditation and spiritual training of the Eastern type we have described in this book is brought out by Alexander d'Agapeyeff in his introduction to the book just quoted. He describes the Jesus Prayer as 'a scientific attempt to change the one who prays'. The full effect is reached when the mental repetition of the prayer becomes effortless and in the place of the heart 'lives *itself* with every heart beat'. As Bishop Brianchaninov says, 'union of heart and mind', and 'prayer filled with divine grace and power'. This is the passage from full attentiveness to effortless contemplation described by Patanjali, the 'Father of Yoga'. 'When the Jesus Prayer is used in this way,' says Alexander d'Agapeyeff, 'the disciple changes himself, remakes himself and becomes a totally different person.'

If the words of the Jesus Prayer are not congenial, another short prayer may be substituted. Remember the story of the dervish who walked on the water.

Before leaving the use of the mantra in Christian contemplative prayer, we should not fail to read a few lines from *The Cloud of Unknowing*, the work of an anonymous monk writing probably in the fourteenth century. He says that any person who seeks 'to be knit to God in spirit, in unity of love, and accordance of will' can develop 'special ways, tricks, private techniques, and spiritual devices' that induce states of deep contemplation. Here is one of the ways: 'Take a short word, preferably of one syllable . . . the shorter the word the better, being more like the meaning of the Spirit: a word like "God" or "love". Choose one which you like, or perhaps some other so long as it is of one syllable. And fix this word fast to your heart, so that it is always there come what may. It will be your shield and spear in peace and war alike. With this word you will suppress all thought under the cloud of forgetting.'

As mentioned earlier, the word chosen as a mantra need not be sacred or even 'one which you like', but may be one with a neutral tone or a word entirely without meaning to the meditator. Repetition of a meaningless Sanskrit sound is the method of Maharshi Mahesh Yogi's Transcendental Meditation, currently widely taught and practised in the West.

Maharishi Mahesh Yogi - the 'Man of la Mantra'

The Maharishi – the title means 'Sage' or 'Wise One' – does not claim that his method of Transcendental Meditation is new. He traces it back to the *Vedas*, the world's oldest scriptures, and he has written a commentary on the *Bhagavad Gita*, written five hundred years before the birth of Christ, linking Transcendental Meditation with that work. He learned the method from his teacher, Swami Brahmananda Saraswati (1869–1953), Shankachayara of the monastery of Jyotir Math, who entrusted him with the task of carrying a simple, easily learned form of it to the world.

He was born Mahesh Prasad Varma at Jubblepore, Central India, in 1918, the son of a forest ranger. His upbringing belonged to conventional Hindu culture. He took a degree in physics at the University of Allahabad in 1942. Much of the success in spreading Transcendental Meditation in the West has been due to its scientific presentation. The Maharishi welcomes investigation by medical scientists and TM's sales literature and books by followers of the Maharishi, with their charts showing galvanic skin responses, blood lactate levels, and patterns of brain wave rhythms, are very different in tone from the majority of books on Hindu and other meditation.

While a university student, the Maharishi met Swami Brahmananda Saraswati and, after taking his degree in physics, he spent thirteen years as a disciple of the Hindu monk. He keeps a picture of the Swami near him at all times, even when giving talks in public. Swami Saraswati, shortly before his death in 1953, told his favourite pupil to perfect and teach a mental technique applicable to everyone everywhere. Maharishi Mahesh Yogi felt ready to teach it after spending two years living as a hermit at Uttar Kashi.

For a few years, the Maharishi taught Transcendental Meditation in India; he then decided that faster progress in spreading the method would be achieved by teaching it in the most technologically advanced nations of the world, and by making full use of modern means of communication. He established the Spiritual Regeneration Movement in America in 1961, and in London in the following year.

The appeal of Transcendental Meditation to Westerners lies in its scientific presentation, its simplicity, and in the fact that the meditator is not asked to change his life style in any way apart from meditating for about twenty minutes morning and evening. It is presented as a technique, not as a religion. The Maharishi's Hindu beliefs are kept in the background. The practice, he says, makes the Hindu a better Hindu, the Buddhist a better Buddhist, the Christian a better Christian – and unbelievers improve the quality of their lives.

While receiving an admiration and respect bordering on reverence from his followers, the Maharishi's personality and scientific approach prevents his receiving the undisciplined and, for western tastes, cloying adoration accorded some Indian gurus; he also makes no claim to miraculous powers (*siddhis*). This has led to most emphasis being placed on Transcendental Meditation as a technique. The method is simple and merely involves the mental repetition of a Sanskrit word or mantra. Western journalists dubbed the Maharishi 'the Man of La Mantra'. Over one million men, women, and children have been taught the method in Europe and in America by trained teachers. There is no way of estimating how many people have taken it up without paying the donation at initiation or being instructed by the official teachers.

What is Transcendental Meditation?

The goal of Transcendental Meditation is that common to all mystical systems of meditation: the uncovering of pure consciousness and being. The Maharishi's method is to inwardly repeat a Sanskrit word, a thought, so that conscious awareness penetrates from a gross state of thought to ever more subtler states of thought, and eventually to the source of thought. This is the state of bliss consciousness, which is the state of pure existence. There we tap a rich reservoir of energy and intelligence, says the Maharishi.

Meditative attention is the tool employed by TM, as it is often called. 'In transcendental meditation,' the Maharishi explained on American television, 'the attention comes from outside to the inside, to the source of thought; and then the conscious mind, the awareness in the waking state of consciousness, gains that transcendent pure awareness which is bliss consciousness . . . It is just thinking, but thinking in a manner so that awareness goes deep within and gains that inner being of pure consciousness.'

Awareness is taken inwards to pure existence by mentally repeating a meaningless Sanskrit word of one or two syllables, while the meditator sits motionless (on a chair will do) with the eyes closed. The mantra is not forced to stay in the mind. Thoughts and images inevitably arise, but after a little practice awareness that one is thinking leads automatically to returning to repetition of the mantra.

The mantra is a thought-sound that takes attention to the source of thought. It is repeated inwardly without moving the organs of speech. The instructor tells the meditator not to try. It seems to me that trying not to try is still trying, but in practice the problem soon lapses. Once a person has known the flow of meditative awareness, it will reappear automatically, like the balancing skill in riding a bicycle.

The Maharishi goes against Hindu cultural tradition in trusting in the mechanical repetition of the mantra and not asking that devotional meaningfulness be imprinted on each repetition. The mind is naturally drawn to the depths where bliss consciousness is found, to the field of pure consciousness. So let the mantra do its work, says the Maharishi. Sometimes it will be in conscious awareness and sometimes it will have slipped out of mind. During some of the time the mantra is absent it will be supplanted by thoughts and images. These are signs that stress is being released from the nervous system and body. At other times the mantra will slip away and be replaced by pure awareness and being, the transcendental fourth state of consciousness beyond the states of dreamless sleep, dreaming sleep, and ordinary waking consciousness. Because this is a state of nothing-ness the dichotomies of subject-object and experiencer-experienced are transcended. As consciousness rests within itself, paradoxically you can only know that you have been there on returning to the surface levels of consciousness. The quality of relaxation and rest in depth makes the meditator aware that he has contacted pure being. The Maharishi likens the process of transcendental meditation to diving from the surface turbulence of an ocean to its silent and peaceful depths.

In TM you meditate for forty minutes a day, in two periods of twenty minutes, separated by at least six hours of activity. You wait at least two hours following a meal before meditating. Morning and evening make the most suitable times for meditation. Otherwise there is no need to change one's life-style in any way; this is a feature of the Maharishi's teaching that has aroused opposition from other Indian gurus. According to the Maharishi, life-styles change spontaneously under the influence of regular meditation. The alternation of deep rest in meditation twice daily with normal activity during the other hours of the day leads to everyday activity becoming infused with the qualities of pure being. When, usually after some years of meditation, pure being becomes permanently established for twenty-four hours a day, the state is called Cosmic Consciousness. Yoga, Sufism, Zen and other systems of meditation aim also for this attainment of permanently transformed being, sometimes called 'universal man'.

One Man One Mantra?

A controversial feature of Transcendental Meditation is the claim that there is a specific mantra whose vibrations match those of each initiate. The instructors are told how to select a mantra to suit each meditator as part of their teacher-training course. The applicant is interviewed and fills in a questionnaire, on the basis of which a mantra is selected. The 'special, personal mantra' is revealed following the initiation ceremony.

Initiation involves a ceremony that contrasts a little strangely with the otherwise scientific and Westernised presentation of TM. The applicant is asked to bring some symbolic offerings to the ceremony: flowers (representing the flower of life), fruit (representing the seed of life), and a spotlessly-clean white handkerchief (representing cleansing of the spirit). The ceremony takes place in a softly-lit room, filled with the fragrance of burning incense. There are pictures of Maharishi Mahesh Yogi and of his master, Swami Saraswati, whom the Maharishi calls Guru Dev. The instructor goes through a ten-minute ceremony in which he or she recites Sanskrit words and handles rice, salt, and sandalwood. Practising Christians sometimes have qualms about the ceremony, but Transcendental Meditation is not a religion and the initiation ceremony is mainly a way of saying 'thank you' to the teachers of the method. The use of a Sanskrit word as mantra ensures that it has no specific meaning known to Western meditators.

The meditator is told by the teacher not to divulge the personal mantra to any other person, not even to a husband or wife. As there are more people starting Transcendental Meditation than there are Sanskrit mantras, some mantras are shared, occasionally even by husbands and wives. Some meditators find the sound of the word given to them awkward to pronounce. Adam Smith (G. J. W. Goodman), in *Powers of Mind* (W. H. Allen), reports that he was given the mantra SHIAM – a more awkward sound than he had expected from his knowledge of Sanskrit Hindu mantras such as OM, HUM, or BAM. He was assured that this was the right mantra to suit his vibrations.

A point arises about the neutrality of the sound. Whilst the Sanskrit mantras used in Transcendental Meditation are meaningless in themselves, to the Westerners who use them, they often bear resemblances to words in English and in other European languages. Thus in the example just given – SHIAM – one might easily associate the sound with words like 'Siam', 'shame', 'sham',

'Sam', 'she am', 'Shiah', and so on. In practice, however, the words are sufficiently neutral for their few possible associations not to be troublesome, except perhaps very early in learning meditation. A meditator who reports his experiences of learning TM in the book *Tranquillity Without Pills* (Peter H. Wyden, USA; Souvenir Press, London) found that the mantra he was given resembled the name of a friend of his wife's.

Maharishi Mahesh Yogi likens finding the right mantra for each meditator to making sure a blood infusion is of the right group. However, the analogy is very exaggerated and investigations into the use of mantras carried out at Harvard Medical School appear to show that it is the repetition under the correct conditions of meditation that produce valuable results and not the potency of the vibrations of the word that is used. People had discovered this many years before.

Early in life Alfred, Lord Tennyson – England's most celebrated Victorian poet – found the basic technique of Mantra Yoga and Transcendental Meditation to be, according to a letter he wrote to a Mr. B. P. Blood: 'a kind of waking trance – this for lack of a better word – I have frequently had, quite up from boyhood, when I have been all alone. This has come upon me through repeating my own name to myself silently, till all at once, as it were out of the intensity of the consciousness of individuality, individuality itself seemed to dissolve and fade away into boundless being, and this is not a confused state but the clearest, the surest of the surest, utterly beyond words – where death was an almost laughable impossibility – the loss of personality (if so it were) seeming no extinction, but the only true life. I am ashamed of my feeble description. Have I not said the state is utterly beyond words?'

Tennyson would appear to have known the pure being that results from surrender of the ego and its conditioned encrustations – that is, he had hit on a form of the Onion Game described in Chapter 8, using his own name as a mantra for silent repetition of the kind favoured in Transcendental Meditation. The result was not the 'blank mind' that many people fear in such an exercise. Professor John Tyndall recorded that the poet said of this mantra-induced state of mind: 'By God Almighty! there is no delusion in the matter! It is no nebulous ecstasy, but a state of transcendent wonder, associated with absolute clearness of mind.'

Dr. Richard Maurice Bucke, in *Cosmic Consciousness*, first published in Philadelphia in 1901, quotes Tennyson's letter and comments:' *"Repeating my own name"*. Tennyson quite unconsciously was using the means laid down from immemorial time for the attainment of illumination. "He who thinking of nothing, making the mind cease to work, adhering to uninterrupted meditation, *repeating the single syllable OM*, meditating on me, reached the highest goal" (Bhagavad Gita). Of course it makes no difference what word or name is used. What is required is that the action of the mind should be as far as possible suspended, especially that all desires of every kind be stilled, nothing wished or feared, the mind in perfect health and vigour, but held quiescent in a state of calm equipoise.' Dr. Bucke himself was familiar with heightened states of consciousness.

Dr. Bucke's view – *'of course it makes no difference what word or name is used*' – received scientific confirmation seventy years later. In Chapter 2 we described Dr. Herbert Benson's investigation of how meditation elicits what he calls the Relaxation Response, in which there are pronounced physiological and psychological changes. In his book *The Relaxation Response* (William Morrow, New York) he states clearly and emphatically: 'It is important to remember that there is not a single method that is unique in eliciting the Relaxation Response. For example, Transcendental Meditation is one of the many techniques that incorporate these components of effective meditation. However, we believe it is not necessary to use the specific method and specific *secret*, personal sound taught by Transcendental Meditation. Tests at the Thorndike Memorial Laboratory of Harvard have shown that a similar technique used with any sound or phrase or prayer or mantra brings forth the same physiologic changes noted during Transcendental Meditation: decreased oxygen consumption; decreased carbon-dioxide elimination; decreased rate of breathing. In other words, using the basic necessary components, any of the age-old or the newly derived techniques produces the same physiological results regardless of the mental device used.'

Dr. Una Kroll, in *TM: A Signpost for the World* (Darton,

Longman and Todd), an assessment of transcendental meditation from a Christian point of view, says: 'At least one person known to me has substituted a Christian "mantra" for the given Sanskrit one, and apparently learnt the technique to the satisfaction of the teacher who never knew what his pupil had done.' I have myself been told of several cases of meditators changing their mantras for other reasons. One person found that the Sanskrit word given to him resembled the name of a divorced wife whom he wished to forget: he pressurised a friend into divulging his 'secret' mantra and used that. Fortunately, it was not a duplication of his own mantra. In another case, the meditator had been for some years using the famous 'primary mantra' OM and found it difficult to introduce another word; he therefore stayed with OM and practised it in the TM manner. In each case, the instructor had no inkling that the 'secret, personal mantra' was not being used.

Whatever view one takes on the question of whether or not TM instructors can really select the most effective mantra for each individual, there is still much in the service given that might persuade an individual to pay the initiation donation, although the sum concerned is not inconsiderable.

The introductory talks, the initiation ceremony, and the follow-up checking sessions have practical and psychological value. It is well known that ritual and expectation help in making any technique or therapy effective. Doctors and psychotherapists do not hesitate to use them. William C. Coe and Linda G. Buckner, in *Helping People Change* (Pergamon General Psychology Series, Volume 52) say: 'The importance of a person's expectations for the outcome of treatment has long been recognised. Similarities among healers from many persuasions, including witchdoctors and psychotherapists, have been pointed out, and the importance of expectations may overshadow effects of the treatments they claim to administer. Drugs and other therapies appear at times to be no more effective than the patient's "faith" in the treatment. These curative effects are often called "placebo" effects, indicating they are not specific to the "treatment" effects. They exist nevertheless, sometimes to a remarkable degree, and should therefore be considered in administering helping procedures.' These writers discuss the use of suggestive techniques in teaching relaxation and concentration, in autogenic training, and in the practice of Yoga meditation. Maharishi Mahesh Yogi is confident that the physiological changes and altered consciousness produced by transcendental meditation are not due to auto-suggestion or auto-hypnosis, and that the changes will occur even for the sceptic. The studies by Dr. Benson and others seem to bear this out. The introductory talks, the initiation ceremony, and the question and answer checking sessions do however induce high expectation in most people and, if nothing else, serve to take people through the early stages of becoming used to meditation. There is sometimes a feeling, especially in meditations that do not go very well, that it is a waste of time. The knowledge that studies of meditators have come up with positive results in improved health, energy, social harmony, and interpersonal relations adds motivation and confidence.

Practical help is provided by the instructor, who teaches the technique of meditation and is available for consultation over problems that may arise. The problems of meditators have been closely studied and question and answer sheets are filled in by the meditator on post-initiation visits to the teacher. Here are some of the questions, as given in *Tranquillity Without Pills*: 'How many times have you meditated since your last checking?' 'Did you feel that the time during meditation passed quickly?' 'Did you at any moment find that you were unaware of body and surroundings?' 'Did you at moments feel some happiness within?' 'Did thoughts disturb you?' 'During meditation did you notice any change in breathing?' 'Approximately how many times did you lose the mantra during meditation?' 'Do you remember moments when there were no mantra and no thoughts?' 'After meditation do you feel inclined to rest or do you feel energetic?' 'Do you now feel you have understood how to meditate?'

Transcendental Meditation is a *movement*, which you can help if you wish. There are courses and seminars. TM even has its own university.

Transcendental Meditation does have its unknown percentage of drop-outs, but those few surveys that have been carried out indicate that a large majority of initiates continue to meditate daily, months and years after learning the technique. This is a sure sign that the mental technique works. So do other methods.

How one meditates is more important than the choice of object used for meditating upon.

There is a Hindu story which has a similar theme to the Sufi story about the dervish who mispronounced YA HU. A man approached a great Yogi and asked by what method he could attain enlightenment. The guru said: 'Chant RAMA (one of the Hindu names of God) a thousand times a day.'

Many years passed before the two men met again. The great Yogi immediately perceived that the other was enlightened. 'Did you chant the sacred name, as I instructed?' asked the teacher. 'Yes, Master!' came the reply. 'I became a solitary in the mountains, and every day for ten years I chanted MARA MARA MARA a thousand times, just as you told me to do.'

Mara, an anagram of Rama, is the name of the devil!

Maharishi Mahesh Yogi has performed a valuable service in introducing meditation to so many people in the West and in interesting medical scientists in its effects. Valuable too has been the way he has streamlined Mantra Yoga, reducing meditation to its bare essentials, lopping off unnecessary concepts, rituals and exercises. His reiteration that meditation should be effortless is helpful, for passive awareness is the key factor in eliciting the Relaxation Response.

The Maharishi believes that mentally repeating a word is the most direct path to realising 'the field of Being'. But his basic method of moving from a gross thought to a progressively finer thought and eventual transcendence belongs to every method described in this book, whether it be through seeing, listening, touching, feeling, or loving. He acknowledged this himself in *The Science of Being and Art of Living* (SRM Publications). After giving the example of progressive refinement of gazing upon and visualising an object, in the manner of the *kasina* meditations we described in Chapter 6, he says: 'Likewise, through any sense of perception we could begin to experience an object and arrive at the transcendental state of being.'

Maharishi Mahesh Yogi shows great shrewdness in using for transcendental meditation a mentally repeated word, for silent verbalising is at the heart of thought. The silently repeated mantra is therefore an excellent tool for going beyond thought to pure awareness. However, other methods are also effective in reaching pure consciousness. They have been described in this book. One technique, found productive, may be employed – or two or more may be combined in efficacious harmony.

11

Combining Methods

1. *Meditate in a place where distractions of noise, voices, and so on are within your tolerance level.*
2. *Sit motionless, poised, and comfortable.*
3. *Breathe quietly, gently, smoothly, and rhythmically. Breathe through the nostrils and down into the abdomen.*
4. *Combine two or more of the methods described in Chapters 4 to 10. Loving attention and visual or listening meditation go together very naturally. Very conducive to deep relaxation and pure awareness is the combination of mindfulness of abdominal breathing and mental repetition of a word. Produce the word once to each exhalation. Focus awareness on the slight movements of the abdomen a little below the navel.*
5. *Observe a relaxed and passive attitude towards distractions, including thoughts and images that flit in and out of the mind. When you become conscious that your attention has wandered, bring it gently back to the central act of meditation. Do this as many times as is necessary, maintaining the relaxed and passive attitude.*

With the preceding account of the method of repeating a word or phrase (a *mantra*) we conclude our survey of methods of sitting meditation which offer the possibility of personal use without a teacher, during which we have looked at and drawn upon the practices of Hinduism, Taoism, Zen, Christianity, and Sufism, and discussed Transcendental Meditation, an updated streamlined version of one of the practices of Mantra Yoga. Stripped to their basic mechanics, there are the practices of awareness or mindfulness of breathing, gazing upon and/or visualising an object, resting attention upon a sound, stripping the ego of its skins until only the essential Self remains, the way of loving attention, and finally the repetition, aloud and/or mentally, of a *mantra*, a word, phrase, or sound.

Readers have been invited to experiment and to discover which method or methods suit them best and are most productive of the response they are looking for. A single method may be followed, or a combination of two or more methods.

Combining methods sometimes occurs naturally. Loving attention, for example, naturally combines with any of the other techniques. When combined with visual meditations, love is poured into the object gazed upon or visualised, and love adds warmth and resonance to the repetition of *mantras*.

An Effective Combination

An effective combination is to bring together two methods that are suitable for use by *all* meditators, regardless of credal affiliations – they conveniently and easily meet the basic requirements for meditation that produce changes in body and in consciousness. The two techniques are awareness or mindfulness of breathing and repetition of a *mantra*, preferably a single word of one or two syllables.

The first publicity about Transcendental Meditation came along at a time when I had for some years been very satisfactorily practising mindfulness of breathing. However, I was tempted to try mental repetition of a word and also found that very effective. In both methods my attitude had been that of passive awareness, without any judgments over the inevitable entry into my mind of random thoughts and images. Each time I became aware that I was thinking, I returned automatically to the breathing or to the *mantra*. There was no attempt to force results – indeed as I meditated I let things flow and had no thought of results, though they came insofar as they affected the quality of living.

Still having a sense of loss at dropping a much-loved method of meditating and finding my attention often turning to the movements of my abdominal muscles when I was supposed to be using the *mantra*, I then hit on bringing the two methods together, repeating my *mantra* (a Japanese word) on each exhalation of breath, which seemed more natural than saying it on the inhalation, mindful all the while of the act of breathing as recorded by the ocean-like rise and fall of the abdomen. My sensory awareness was in fact centred on that spot a couple of inches or so below the navel which the Japanese call the *tanden* or 'vital centre'. So I was really combining three methods of meditation, though for a time I looked on my method as being twofold.

I practised in this way for several years before coming across Dr. Herbert Benson's *The Relaxation Response* (William Morrow, New York). It was with great interest that I discovered that Dr. Benson was using repetition of a *mantra* plus awareness of breathing very successfully with patients at the Beth Israel Hospital of Boston. You sit comfortably, close your eyes, relax your muscles from toes to face, and become aware of your breathing as you inhale and exhale through the nostrils. Then, as you breathe out, you say 'ONE' in your mind. 'ONE' remains the sole *mantra* – you do not count up to 'ten' as practised widely in the East. You breathe in and out, saying 'ONE'; in . . . out, 'ONE', and so on. You continue for ten to twenty minutes, peeping at a clock occasionally if you wish. Dr. Benson has said that a passive attitude is probably the most important of the components for meditation that elicits the Relaxation Response. So he advises that distracting thoughts should not be given any importance and the meditation should flow at its own pace. He does not specify a localised focus for awareness of breathing and presumably allows the sensation to be generalised. There are no religious associations. Of his 'noncultic technique', Dr. Benson says: 'we claim no innovation but simply a scientific validation of age-old wisdom.'

Mu

Katsuki Sekida, in his *Zen Training* (John Weatherhill, New York and Tokyo), gives detailed instruction for combining awareness of the breath with inward repetition of 'MU', which traditionally is the first *koan* or problem given to students of Zen. It means 'nothing' or 'no-thing'. 'MU' is repeated mentally on an exhalation, either as a series of separate syllables – 'MU,

MU, MU, MU' – or as a constant wavelike drone – 'M-U-U-U-U.' You do not think of the meaning of '*Mu*', but 'take it as the sound of your breath'. After a time you 'look into the *tanden*' – the belly just below the navel. 'It is as if you are going into the depths of the sea,' says Katsuki Sekida, 'ultimately to settle on the bottom of it.' The in and out flow of breath has almost stopped. 'At this stage, if one stops saying "MU" and enters the state in which one is holding and watching the *tanden*, one's practice may be called *shikantaza*. This is not a state of absent-mindedly sitting; it is a wakeful condition.'

Shikantaza is the Soto Zen meditation of 'just sitting' – the freest of all meditations, yet difficult for the beginner.

Katsuki Sekida tells his readers and pupils to avoid 'too stiff and inflexible' an approach to his instructions on meditation. 'Eventually,' he says, 'you will find that you have developed your own style.'

I have the same advice for readers of *Teach Yourself Meditation*. Explore the methods of meditation described in the preceding pages. You will be rewarded with rich discoveries. Develop your own style. Find the methods that work best for you and are most congenial to you. Combine methods, if you wish. Do not be rigid or inflexible.

More than seven hundred years ago the Chinese Ch'an (Zen) master Mumon wrote:

> '*The great path has no gate,*
> *Thousands of roads enter it,*
> *When one passes through this gateless gate*
> *He walks freely between heaven and earth.*'

Bibliography

Anonymous (14th century), trans. C. Wolters, *The Cloud of Unknowing*, Penguin Books, 1961.

Bachofen, J. J., 'An Essay on Mortuary Symbolism', cited Stewart, T. C., *The City as an Image of Man*, Latimer Press, 1970.

Benson, M.D., Herbert, *The Relaxation Response*, William Morrow, New York, 1976; Collins, London, 1976.

The Bhagavad Gita. See Sastri, A. M.

Blyth, R. H., *Zen in English Literature and Oriental Classics*, Hokuseido, Tokyo, 1948; Dutton, New York, 1960.

Brianchaninov, Ignatius, *The Prayer of Jesus*, Stuart and Watkins, 1965.

Brunton, Paul, *The Secret Path*, Rider, 1932; *The Quest for the Overself*, Rider, 1937.

Bucke, R. M., *Cosmic Consciousness*, Philadelphia, 1901.

Butler, Dom Cuthbert, *Western Mysticism*, Constable 1922; 3rd edition 1967.

Chuang Tzu, tr. H. A. Giles, *Chuang-tze, Mystic, Moralist, and Social Reformer*, Quaritch, London, 1889.

Coe, William C. and Buckner, Linda G., in *Helping People Change*, Pergamon General Psychology Series, New York, 1975.

Dvivedi, M. N., trans. *The Yoga Sutras of Patanjali*, Madras, 1890.

Ebon, Martin, ed., *Maharishi, the Guru*, New American Library, New York, 1968.

Evans-Wentz, W. Y., ed., *The Tibetan Book of the Dead,* Oxford University Press, 1927.

Feild, Reshad, *The Last Barrier,* Turnstone Books, 1976.

Ferguson, John, *An Illustrated Encyclopedia of Mysticism and the Mystery Religions,* Thames and Hudson, 1976.

Freuchen, Peter, *Book of the Eskimo,* Fawcett, New York, 1959.

Gollancz, Victor, *My Dear Timothy,* Gollancz, 1952.

Gheranda Samhita. See Vasu, Sris Chandra.

Govinda, Lama Anagarika, *The Way of the White Clouds,* Rider, 1973; *The Middle Way,* August, 1964.

Graham, A.C., trans., *The Book of Lieh Tzu,* John Murray, 1960.

Grou, J. N. (Abbé), *L'Ecole de Jesus Christ,* Thomas Baker, London, 1898.

Happold, F. C., *Mysticism: a Study and an Anthology,* Penguin Books, 1963; *Prayer and Meditation,* Penguin Books, 1971.

Hatha Yoga Pradipika. See Sinh, Pancham.

Hewitt, James, *Yoga,* Teach Yourself Books, 1960; revised and enlarged, 1979; *Yoga and Vitality, Yoga postures, Yoga and Meditation,* Barrie and Jenkins, 1977.

Hirai, Tomio, *Zen Meditation Therapy,* Japan Publications, Tokyo, 1975.

Humphreys, Christmas, *Buddhism,* Penguin Books, 1951; *Zen: A Way of Life,* Teach Yourself Books, 1962.

Jacobson, N. P., *Buddhism: the Religion of Analysis,* Allen and Unwin, 1966.

James, William, *The Varieties of Religious Experience,* Longmans, Green, 1902.

Jefferies, Richard, *The Story of My Heart,* London, 1883.

Kadlovbovsky, E. and Palmer, G. E. H., trans., *Writings from the Philokalia, on the Prayer of the Heart,* Faber and Faber, 1951.

Kapleau, Philip, *The Three Pillars of Zen,* Beacon Press, Boston, 1967.

Khan, Hazrat Inayat, *The Way of Illumination,* The Sufi

Movement, Geneva.

Kroll, Una, TM: *A Signpost for the World*, Darton, Long-man, and Todd, 1974.

Laski, Marghanita, *Ecstasy: A Study of some Secular and Religious Experiences*, Cresset Press, 1961.

Lau, D. C., trans., *Tao Te Ching*, Penguin Books, 1969.

Lewis, C. S., *Surprised by Joy*, Geoffrey Bles, 1955.

Lewis, Howard R. and Streitfeld, Dr. Harold S., *Growth Games*, Souvenir Press, 1972.

Lu K'uan Yü (Charles Luk), *The Secrets of Chinese Meditation*, Rider, 1964.

Lysebeth, Andre van, *Yoga Self Taught*, Harper, New York, 1971; Allen and Unwin, London, 1971.

Mahesh Yogi, Maharishi, *The Science of Being and Art of Living*, SRM Publications, 1963; *On the Bhahagavad Gita*, SRM Publications, 1967; Penguin Books, 1969.

Mangalo, Bhikkhu, *A Manual of the Practice of Recollection*, The Buddhist Society, London, 1970.

Marquès-Rivière, J., *Tantrik Yoga, Hindu and Tibetan*, Rider, undated.

Mascaro, Juan, trans., *The Upanishads*, Penguin Books, 1965.

Maslow, A. H., *Towards a Psychology of Being*, Van Nostrand, Princeton, N.J., 1962.

Menen, Aubrey, *The Space Within the Heart*, Hamish Hamilton, 1970.

Mishra, Ramamurti, *Fundamentals of Yoga*, Julian Press, New York, 1959.

Montague, C. E., *A Writer's Notes on his Trade*, Chatto and Windus, 1930.

The Mother, *Bulletin*, August 1964; Sri Aurobindo Society, Pondicherry.

Muller, Max, tr., *The Upanishads*, Clarendon Press, Oxford, 1898.

Nicholson, R. A., *Mystics of Islam*, Routledge and Kegan Paul, 1966.

Patanjali. See Dvivedi, M. N. and Vivekananda, Swami.

Powys, John Cowper, *A Philosophy of Solitude*, Jonathan

Cape 1933; Village Press, 1974.

Prabhavananda, Swami and Manchester, Frederick, trans., *The Upanishads, Breath of the Eternal*, The Vedanta Society of Southern California, 1957.

Ramana Maharshi, ed. Osborne, Arthur, *The Teachings of Ramana Maharshi*, Rider, 1962.

Robbins, Jhan and Fisher, David, *Tranquillity Without Pills*, Peter H. Wyden, New York, 1972; Souvenir Press, London, 1973.

Ropp, Robert S. de, *The Master Game*, Dell, New York, 1968.

Saint Teresa of Avila, trans. Alice Alexander, *The Way of Perfection*, The Mercier Press, Cork.

Sastri, A. M., trans. *The Bhagavad Gita*, commentary of Sankaracharya, Mysore, 1901.

Scharfstein, Ben-Ami, *Mystical Experience*, Basil Blackwell, 1973.

Scholem, Gershom G., *Jewish Mysticism*, Shocken Books, New York, 1967.

Sekida, Katsuki, *Zen Training*, John Weatherhill, New York, 1975.

Sen, K. M., *Hinduism*, Penguin Books, 1961.

Shankaracharya. See Sastri, A. M.

Shattock, E. H., *An Experiment in Mindfulness*, Rider, 1958.

Sinh, Pancham, trans. *Hatha Yoga Pradipika*, Lalif Moham Bsu, The Panini Office, Allahabad, 1915.

Slade, Herbert, *Exploring into Contemplative Prayer*, Darton, Longman, and Todd, 1975.

Smith, Adam (G. T. W. Goodman), *Powers of Mind*, W. H. Allen, 1976.

Spiegelberg, Frederick, *Spiritual Practices of India*, The Citadel Press, New York, 1962.

Stace, Walter T., *The Teachings of the Mystics*, New American Library, New York, 1960.

Stapleton, Olaf, *Philosophy and Living*, volume 2, Penguin Books, 1939.

Sullivan, J. W. N., *Beethoven: His Spiritual Development*, Alfred A. Knopf, New York, 1927.

Ta-Kao, Ch'u, trans. *Tao Te Ching*, Buddhist Society, London, 1937.

Tagore, Rabindranath, *Sadhana*, Macmillan, 1921.

Trungpa, Chögyam, *Meditation in Action*, Shambal Publications, Berkeley, Cal., 1969; Stuart and Watkins, London, 1969.

Tucci, Giuseppe, trans. Brodrick, A. H., *Theory and Practices of the Mandala*, Rider, 1961.

Underhill, Evelyn, *Mysticism*, Methuen, 1911.

The Upanishads. See Mascaro, Juan, Muller, and Prabhavananda, Swami and Manchester, Frederick.

Vajiranana Mahathera, Paravahera, *Buddhist Meditation in Theory and Practice*, M. D. Gunasena, Colombo, Sri Lanka, 1962.

Vasu, Sris Chandra, trans. *Gheranda Samhita*, Adyar, Madras, 1933.

Vidyarnava, R. B. S. Chandra, trans. *Siva Samhita*, Sudhindra Nath Basu, The Panini Office, Allahabad, 1923.

Vivekananda, Swami, *Raja Yoga, or Conquering the Internal Nature*, Advaita Ashrama, Calcutta, 1901.

Watts, Alan, *The Supreme Identity*, Faber and Faber, 1950; Wildwood House, 1973; *The Way of Zen*, Pantheon Books, New York, 1957; Thames and Hudson, London, 1957; Penguin Books, 1962.

Wei Wu Wei (T. J. Gray), *Open Secret*, Hong Kong University Press, 1965; *The Tenth Man*, Hong Kong University Press, 1966.

Wood, Ernest, *Yoga*, Penguin Books, 1959.

Zwemer, S. M., *A Moslem Seeker After God*, Fleming H. Revell, New York, 1920.

Index

YOGA

JAMES HEWITT

A clear and practical account of Hatha Yoga and Raja Yoga –
the Yogas of bodily health and mental harmony respectively –
whose regular practice produces greater energy, relaxation,
poise and serenity.

The great value of this book is that the broader dimensions of
Yoga are fully considered. A programme of Yoga postures and
breathing exercises, and advice on relaxation and diet, are
followed by a full consideration of Yoga meditation and its
aims. Through regular Yoga practice and meditation you can
attain greater vitality and suppleness, deep psycho-physical
poise and relaxation, serenity and self-realisation.

TEACH YOURSELF BOOKS